11/96

D0442195

PRESENTING
Laurence Yep

Twayne's United States Authors Series
Young Adult Authors

Patricia J. Campbell, General Editor

TUSAS 656

LAURENCE YEP
Photograph by K. Yep

PRESENTING

Laurence Yep

Dianne Johnson-Feelings

Twayne Publishers
An Imprint of Simon & Schuster Macmillan
New York

Prentice Hall International
London Mexico City New Delhi Singapore Sydney Toronto

Twayne's United States Authors Series No. 656

Presenting Laurence Yep
Dianne Johnson-Feelings

Copyright © 1995 by Twayne Publishers

Twayne Publishers
An Imprint of Simon & Schuster Macmillan
866 Third Avenue
New York, NY 10022

Library of Congress Cataloging-in-Publication Data

Johnson-Feelings, Dianne.
    Presenting Laurence Yep / Dianne Johnson-Feelings
        p.   cm. — (Twayne's United States authors series.   Young adult authors)
    Includes bibliographical references and index.
    Summary: Provides biographical information about this Chinese-American award-winning writer and presents literary criticism of some of his works for young adults.
    ISBN 0-8057-8201-X
    1. Yep, Laurence—Juvenile literature.   2. Young adult fiction, American—History and criticism—Juvenile literature.   3. Authors, American—20th century—Biography—Juvenile literature.   4. Chinese-Americans—Biography—Juvenile literature.   [1. Yep, Laurence. 2. Authors, American.   3. Chinese-Americans—Biography.]   I. Title. II. Series.
    PS3575.E6Z73   1995
    813'.54—dc20   95–10307
    [B]   CIP
                                                                                      AC

The paper used in this publication meets the minimum requirements of American National Standard for Information Sciences—Permanence of Paper for Printed Library Materials, ANSI Z39.48-1984. ∞ ™

10 9 8 7 6 5 4 3 2 1

Printed in the United States of America

For Andrea Makapugay, Tillie Lim, and Emily San Jose

Contents

Foreword

The advent of Twayne's Young Adult Authors Series in 1985 was a response to the growing stature and value of adolescent literature and the lack of serious critical evaluation of the new genre. The first volume of the series was heralded as marking the coming-of-age of young adult fiction.

The aim of the series is twofold. First, it enables young readers to research the work of their favorite authors and to see them as real people. Each volume is written in a lively, readable style and attempts to present in an attractive, accessible format a vivid portrait of the author as a person.

Second, the series provides teachers and librarians with insights and background material for promoting and teaching young adult novels. Each of the biocritical studies is a serious literary analysis of one author's work (or one subgenre within young adult literature), with attention to plot structure, theme, character, setting, and imagery. In addition, many of the series writers delve deeper into the creative writing process by tracking down early drafts or unpublished manuscripts by their subject authors, consulting with their editors or other mentors, and examining influences from literature, film, or social movements.

Many of the authors contributing to the series are among the leading scholars and critics of adolescent literature. Some are even novelists for young adults themselves. Most of the studies are based on extensive interviews with the subject author, and each includes an exhaustive study of his or her work. Although the general format is the same, the individual volumes are uniquely shaped by their subjects, and each brings a different perspective to the classroom.

The goal of the series is to produce a succinct but comprehensive study of the life and art of every leading writer for young adults to trace how that art has been accepted by readers and critics, and to evaluate its place in the developing field of adolescent literature. And—perhaps most important—the series is intended to inspire a reading and rereading of this quality fiction that speaks so directly to young people about their life experiences.

PATRICIA J. CAMPBELL, GENERAL EDITOR

Preface

Laurence Yep understands both people and books. His doctoral program, in fact, combined the study of psychology and literature. This seems a fitting focus for someone who spent so much of his early life reading and observing people in his family's store. Now, as a writer, he enjoys the many audiences that enjoy his work. For instance, he animatedly tells me the story of watching a group of students at a theatrical production of *Dragonwings*. During the scene in which Moon Shadow has tea with his new friend, Mrs. Whitlaw, he refers to the gingerbread cookies she serves as "dung." One boy in the audience leans over to ask his teacher the meaning of the word. Giggling, he shares the information with a classmate, and a ripple effect moves through the audience. Yep laughs, "So I guess in a way we had expanded their vocabulary."

No matter how silly this story may seem, in some ways it gets to the heart of what Laurence Yep's work is about. In all of his books, he is interested in some way in the power of words and in the idea of translation—attaining and using various languages to negotiate one's way through this world, being able to read people and situations as well as words. His own experience with languages and communicating is interesting. He can read Latin and Greek, but he has never become fluent in Chinese, which has, at times, made him feel like an outsider even with his own family members or in San Francisco's Chinatown. On the other hand, white Americans have often made him and many others feel like outsiders only because they are Chinese Americans.

Consequently, Laurence Yep has always been interested in the experiences of those he identifies as outsiders and survivors, and it is to them that he thinks his writing appeals most. An indelible encounter was with a young boy resistant to Yep's comments until they learned that they shared an interest in Godzilla movies, as evident in *Kind Hearts and Gentle Monsters*. When Yep asked the young man what it was he liked about Godzilla, he answered that "he's big and clumsy and no one explains the rules to him." Yep feels that this description applies not only to those typically thought of as outsiders, but to teenagers in general. In his own words, adolescents are "outsiders in their own bodies." No wonder that his young adult books are so popular. Not only does he understand the audience, but he offers them strategies for surviving, for living through the small and big moments. He considers nothing—no thought, no action, no predicament—insignificant.

Laurence Yep is prolific and the winner of some of the most prestigious awards in the world of publishing. He is the author of short stories, novels, picture books, essays, screenplays, and an autobiography. He is an anthologist as well. He writes science fiction, fantasy, historical fantasy, historical fiction, and contemporary realism. Especially, he draws upon and interprets Chinese mythology as he chronicles Chinese-American experience. But no matter the subject matter, he is a meticulous researcher and an inspired storyteller.

Perhaps above all, Laurence Yep is a person. He reminds me, in fact, of the Shell Woman's husband in *The Shell Woman and the King*, "a good man . . . whom everyone liked and who liked everyone."[1] When I conducted my first interview with him, in the spring of 1993, we met in a café in the section of San Francisco where he lives with his wife Joanne. A writer and editor herself, she is one of the people responsible for Yep's first getting published. They met during his time as a student at Marquette University, one of his many experiences of functioning in a cultural community removed from his Chinese-American background. But he has always lived life in a kind of multicultural way, a theme that is interwoven throughout his autobiography.

Part of what strikes me about him is his unassuming manner and appearance. He has a boyish, yet intense air about him. Hair sweeping across his forehead, wearing glasses and plain clothes, he is a fun-loving intellectual who relishes good conversation. He talks to me, half-jokingly, about authors who have taken on the persona of The Writer—people he can imagine entering a room wearing a cape and hat. But Yep himself, never. Bill Morris, an executive at HarperCollins, has told me that Laurence Yep is a publishing company's dream, interacting well with those in every department there. It is because he is humane that his writing is so powerful and says so much to so many different readers.

In this presentation of Laurence Yep, I will not attempt to discuss his life and work exhaustively. It is a daunting task even to attempt to write about the life of a person who has written his autobiography recently, and engagingly. It is daunting as well to write about such a prolific author, whose body of work seems to expand as rapidly as each new volume can be read. Because this series focuses on young adult literature, what I will attempt to offer here is the introduction and analysis of Laurence Yep's books classified as specifically for teenagers. The rest of his work, and his autobiography, will stand as backdrops to provide the larger context for his accomplishments as a whole.

I thank my editor, Patty Campbell, for encouraging me to take on this project. I thank Catherine ("Missy") Lewis for being an especially efficient and congenial editorial assistant. Both of these women gave me invaluable feedback at various stages of the writing process. My appreciation goes to Bill Morris of HarperCollins for his enthusiastic support of the book and to Charlotte Zolotow, Yep's former editor, and Antonia Markiet, his current editor, for speaking with me. I am grateful, too, to the National Academy of Education and the Spencer Foundation for their financial support during part of time during which I worked on this book. And finally, I am indebted to Laurence Yep for sharing with me hard-to-find documents such as his first science fiction short story, various articles, and unpublished screenplays. More importantly, I thank him for being open to me, an African-American female, doing this book. When I asked him if my writing the book concerned him in any way, he asked only that I do my homework—a responsibility too often neglected by writers engaged in the touchy business of communicating, translating, and interpreting multicultural literature. And it is the literature that is most important of all. For the work itself, I thank Laurence Yep.

I am grateful for permission to use the following previously copyrighted material:

Excerpts from *The Lost Garden*. © 1991 Laurence Yep. Published by Julian Messner, a division of Silver Burdett Press. Used with permission.

"Writing *Dragonwings*," Laurence Yep, *The Reading Teacher*, January 1977, 359–63. Reprinted with permission of the International Reading Association.

"The Green Cord" by Laurence Yep, from *Horn Book*, May–June 1989, reprinted by permission of the Horn Book, Inc.

"A Garden of Dragons" by Laurence Yep. Reprinted by permission of the *ALAN Review*, publication of the Assembly on Literature for Adolescents of the National Council of Teachers of English, and by permission of Laurence Yep.

"A Cord to the Past" by Laurence Yep, *CMLEA Journal*, 15:1 (1991). This journal is the official publication of the California Media and Library Educators Association.

Chronology

1914   Yep's father, Yep Gim Lew, is born in China, Toisan district, Kwangtung province (joining his father in the United States at age ten).

1915   Yep's mother, Franche Lee, is born in Lima, Ohio (and raised in Clarksburg, West Virginia).

1939   Yep's brother, Thomas, is born in San Francisco (nicknamed Spike or Gimlet).

1948   Laurence Michael Yep is born in San Francisco on 14 June (named by his brother).

1966   Yep's senior year of high school at St. Ignatius. Enters Marquette University to study journalism. While there, meets Joanne Ryder, who encourages him to write and publish; they later marry.

1968   Writes "The Selchey Kids," his first science fiction story.

1969   "The Selchey Kids" included in *The World's Best Science Fiction of 1969*.

1970   B.A. from University of California (U.C.), Santa Cruz. First teaching position at the State University of New York (SUNY), Buffalo.

1971   "The Electric Neon Mermaid," in *Quark 2*. "In the Sky of Daemons," in *Protostars*. Teaching Fellowship, SUNY at Buffalo.

1972   "The Looking-Glass Sea," in *Strange Bedfellows*.

1973   *Sweetwater*. "The Eddystone Light," in *Demon Kind*.

1974   Research Fellowship, SUNY at Buffalo. Teaches at San Jose City College and the Mountain View campus of Foothill College.

1975   *Dragonwings*. Ph.D. from SUNY at Buffalo.

1976   *Dragonwings* named a 1976 Newbery Honor Book.

1977   *Child of the Owl* and *Seademons*.

1979   *Sea Glass*.

1981   *The Mark Twain Murders*.

1982   *Kind Hearts and Gentle Monsters*.

1983   *Liar, Liar* and *Dragon of the Lost Sea*.

1984   *The Serpent's Children* and *The Tom Sawyer Fires*.

1985   *Dragon Steel*, *Mountain Light*, and *Shadow Lord*.

1986   *Monster Makers, Inc.*

1987   *The Curse of the Squirrel*. Plays *Pay the Chinaman* and *Fairy Bones* are produced by the Asian-American Theatre Company. Teaches at U.C. Berkeley, Asian-American Studies.

1989   *The Rainbow People*. *Pay the Chinaman* published in *Between Worlds*.

1990   National Endowment for the Arts fellowship.

1991   National Endowment for the Arts fellowship for fiction. *Dragon Cauldron*, *The Lost Garden*, *The Star Fisher*, and *Tongues of Jade*. *Dragonwings* is produced by Berkeley Repertory Theatre, September through December.

1992 *Dragonwings*, the playscript, is published in *American Theatre Magazine* and begins touring nationally. New production by Lincoln Center (fall) and Searle Children's Theatre (1993) and extended national tour. Revised version of *Pay the Chinaman* and *Fairy Bones*, a new version, produced by the Pan-Asian Repertory Theatre.

1993 *American Dragons, Dragon's Gate, The Butterfly Boy*, and *The Man Who Tricked a Ghost*.

1994 *The Ghost Fox, The Shell Woman and the King*, and *The Boy Who Swallowed Snakes. Dragon's Gate* named a 1993 Newbery Honor Book.

1995 Forthcoming: *The Tree of Dreams: Ten Tales from the Garden of Night, Tiger Woman, Later, Gator, Hiroshima*, and *The City of Dragons*.

1. A Garden of Dragons and the Lost Garden: Introducing Laurence Yep

To my surprise, I found it difficult to understand a set of myths where there was no ultimate evil. Instead, the creations of light balance the creations of darkness; and a legendary villain can wind up in Heaven as a bureaucrat.

More importantly, it was hard to reset my mental gyroscopes to enter that Chinese universe. In our western cosmos, the supernatural and the natural are opposing and even antagonistic forces. The fantastical is synonymous with illusion and has no existence in the real world.

However, in a Chinese universe, the supernatural and the natural are simply the different ends of the same spectrum.

Laurence Yep, in "A Garden of Dragons"

Dragon of the Lost Sea

Ever since Laurence Yep sold his first science fiction story, when he was only eighteen years old, it was his intention to use Chinese mythology in both his science fiction and fantasy. It was not until 1980, however, that he found what he considered "the perfect vehicle"—a folktale in which the Monkey King, a central character in Chinese folklore, captures a river spirit who has been responsible for the flooding of an entire village.[1] This river spirit becomes the character Civet in *Dragon of the Lost Sea*. After first conceiving the story in the form of a picture book and after writing six drafts of it as a novel, Yep had only begun the project, for "towards the end of the novel, I introduced two new characters, a dragon and her pet boy. They were such lively characters that they stole whatever scene they were in; and I realize that I had to tear up almost everything and rebuild the story around that dragon called Shimmer and her pet boy" ("Garden," 7). Fans of Laurence Yep are fortunate to have access to this kind of reflection by the writer himself. It reveals so much about the creative process and the personal qualities demanded of a writer of Yep's caliber—perseverance, commitment, discipline, the ability to critique one's own work and yet remain passionate about it.

This story of the constantly evolving friendship between Shimmer and Thorn, the boy, is in some ways about their possessing similar kinds of qualities—virtues they will need as they undertake a shared mission. Thorn's kindness is the quality that Shimmer recognizes during the book's initial scenes when Thorn defends her from the abuse, verbal and physical, of village children. Referring to humans, Shimmer thinks, "it was the first kindness that any one of them had ever done me."[2] But what she admires most about Thorn is his spirit: "His was an attitude of believing that even the smallest, most menial things must be done well. We try to develop just that same kind of spirit when we're young; but it's rare among humans—let alone in a young kitchen servant" (*Lost Sea*, 12). Even more, this is the kind of spirit that encompasses so many other qualities as well. It is the kind of spirit that makes it possible for different kinds of "creatures"—human, dragon—to find some common ground.

Before finding that common ground, though, a lot of Shimmer's preconceptions have to be worked through. For example, she believes that human hearts are, for the most part, "hard and flinty" (*Lost Sea*, 4). She does not trust humans at all, having learned long ago "never to turn my back to them and always to keep the exit within easy reach" (15). And finally, the ultimate marker of her contempt, or at least condescension toward them, is that she thinks that they all look alike: "I always have a hard time telling humans apart—they have almost no features at all: such tiny eyes and such little snouts" (6–7).

Certainly, Shimmer's attitude is suggestive of how people of various groups—whether religious, racial, or of some other kind—approach each other, failing to reach a proper balance between group identity and individual identity. But part of the power of *Dragon of the Lost Sea* is that the primary narrative voice is not human. So every reader, from Shimmer's perspective, is part of the "out-group." Readers do not have the choice of identifying with one subset or another of humans. In Shimmer's world, they are, simply, humans, a designation that carries, from the beginning of the story, negative connotations.

As the story opens, Shimmer is in disguise as she wanders the Earth, cast into exile by her fellow dragons of the Lost Sea. Her being attired as an elderly human beggar woman makes her subject to the abuse and whims of humans, who make distinctions among themselves and label her an outsider. They inform her that "the times are so bad we barely manage to take care of our own" and admonish her to be on her way (*Lost Sea*, 6). But after some pleading, a village guard allows her to try her luck. Her reaction is: "I forced myself to smile and bow my head gratefully. (Of all the things I have had to learn to do among humans, I think bowing my head has been the hardest—especially when the favor done me is no favor at all.)" (6). Interestingly enough, at this point in the book, readers do not know the protagonist's name or that she is a dragon, although they may make assumptions based on the book's title. So even if Shimmer's identity is not a revelation to readers, it certainly is for the boy Thorn, coming well past the opening of the story.

The information is revealed only after a series of events culminating in Shimmer's rescue of Thorn from the magic of Civet, the "great enemy of [her] clan" (*Lost Sea*, 7). During the episode, Shimmer thinks "that it was sheer madness to defend a human boy. It was more important to take care of my own kind" (25). And who is her kind? In her words: "My people are the oldest and best of all living creatures" (35). Not only is she a dragon, but a dragon princess—one reason that she may not like bowing her head in humility. What is apparent is that the conflict in this

story is not only between dragons and humans. Humans discriminate against one another—it is from a human mouth that the
phrase "own kind" comes, referring to caste distinctions. The
dragons, too, have a well-delineated class system.

These tensions and divisions can be overcome, though. And in
essence, *Dragon of the Lost Sea* is about the struggle to cross
these barriers, to make the friendship between Shimmer and
Thorn real and enduring. The development of their relationship
is helped by their each being an outsider of a kind. Thorn is an
indentured servant with no relatives. Shimmer is in exile. And at
least to Thorn, "the thought of being alone in the world seemed
far more frightening than Civet and his ally, the Keeper, a
wicked wizard—who still seemed partly imaginary" (*Lost Sea*,
46). He expresses repeatedly throughout the novel his feeling
that "everyone needs someone—even if it's only to scratch their
back" (50).

Part of why Civet and the Keeper seem partly imaginary to
Thorn is that they are magical and mystical. He can only speculate about them as he prepares to battle them as Shimmer's partner in restoring and being restored as a member of the Lost Sea
community. The partnership is being negotiated constantly, analyzed constantly. At one point, Shimmer admonishes Thorn that
"we are not a team. . . . To be a teammate you must be an equal
partner" (*Lost Sea*, 63). Admonishing herself for her negative
feelings toward the boy after they have survived quite a few
ordeals together, she thinks: "And yet loyalty ought to count for
something in this wicked world" (100). At a moment when Thorn
calls out to Shimmer, almost sobbing, fearing that she might be
dead, Shimmer confesses: "I was startled for a moment, since I
don't think there was anyone else in this world who cared
whether I was alive or dead" (160).

There are other moments, though, when each partner doubts
the integrity of the companion. For example, when Thorn finds it
necessary, to save their lives, to pretend he has betrayed
Shimmer, Shimmer thinks the worst: "Well, I thought to myself
bitterly, so much for the promise he had made when he had first
asked to go with me. At that time, he had said that he would

never let me down; and during our long journey, I had actually begun to have faith in him. But now I knew he was just as treacherous and deceitful as the rest of his kind" (*Lost Sea*, 178). But eventually, faith supersedes doubt. And readers are compelled to think about notions such as loyalty, caring, equality, sacrifice, love, history, humor, and dreaming.

Critic Denise M. Wilms appreciates the balanced tone of the book. In particular, she points out that Yep decides "to turn the wily Civet into a victim as well as a villain." Not only does Shimmer come to trust Thorn, but surprisingly, allies with Civet as well. Wilms recognizes that "Shimmer's final choice not to destroy Civet represents a compassionate moral choice that gives the book substance above that of entertaining adventure."[3]

Yep expertly weaves together an adventure story, one full of fights and battles and descriptions of hostile environments and alien enemies. But perhaps most important, the fight all of the characters are engaged in is the fight for security—represented by *home*. Shimmer can empathize with Civet after realizing that Civet, like herself, had lost her home. When Thorn asks whether or not she went home after gaining her freedom from the River King, Civet responds this way: "There wasn't any home to go back to. . . . When I swam back, I found all the old mat huts had been replaced by buildings of pink stone, and the long pilings of the wharves had sunk into the riverbank like fangs. I could hardly even see the sunlight because of all the horrid chemicals and filth in the water" (*Lost Sea*, 196).

Importantly, despite Civet's disillusionment about the destruction of her home due to disregard for the environment and Shimmer's complaints about family dynamics, Thorn still wants both a home and a family. So it is momentous when Shimmer finally declares: "Well, we're family in a strange sort of way. I mean, heaven knows where my clan is because they're scattered all around the world, and you're an orphan. . . . And we already seem to have adopted one another." The conversation unfolds with Thorn's questioning Shimmer's sincerity, asking her if she is sure about the "adoption." When Shimmer answers that she is sure, Thorn admits, "I suppose I am [sure] too, . . . so I guess we're related after all" (*Lost Sea*, 209). The characters know more about friendship, about the meaning of home, and about themselves. With this newfound stability in the relationship and their growing maturity, the friends are ready to confront any obstacles as their struggle continues in *Dragon Steel*, *Dragon Cauldron*, and *Dragon War*, in which Yep chronicles the many physically fierce confrontations between various characters of many worlds.

In addition to the story of the Monkey King, the mythological tale of the Old Mother of the Waters inspired *Dragon of the Lost Sea*. But in his afterword, Yep reminds his readers that "stories—like people—develop and grow, so only a few images have survived from the first version of this novel" (*Lost Sea*, 213). And in this series, the stories grow and develop in marvelous, magical, and fantastical ways. He creates in effect an entire universe, which he himself enjoys: "It wasn't simply writing the story but creating the universe of the books that I've come to enjoy."[4] In the words of Margaret A. Chang, it is a universe filled with "harrowing captures; hairsbreadth escapes; clever ruses; vast battles on air, land, and sea; heroic sacrifices; and dizzying . . . shape changes."[5] All this is facilitated by Yep's remaining true to the spirit of the Chinese mythology he employs, a mythology that acknowledges various realities and truths while not being constrained by details.

It is this spirit that is of paramount importance. And in some significant ways, Chinese dragon mythology and by extension Yep's dragon stories are quite different from those with which some readers are familiar. Critic Joel Taxel notes that "Yep's conception of dragons as noble and heroic is an interesting departure from their villainous portrayal in much of western folklore and fantasy."[6] Reviewer Hanna B. Zeiger places Yep's work in the context of others' books: "For readers who have enjoyed the dragon worlds created by Anne McCaffrey and Jane Yolen, which are rooted in Western tradition, Yep's dragon kingdom with its background of Chinese myths will be a welcome addition."[7] What Zeiger calls the dragon kingdom, what Yep calls "a garden of dragons," is a welcome addition not only to "dragon books" but to children's literature as a whole (though several reviewers point out that the story line can be confusing to readers who are not familiar with the entire series). And though these books, as fantasies, represent only one category of Yep's large body of writing, the spirit with which they are imbued permeates his entire body of work. It is a spirit that is Chinese. But just as significantly, it is a spirit that is expansive and inclusive, accommodating of contradictions, challenging and balanced.

The Lost Garden

The spirit of the Dragon series is Laurence Yep's spirit—the spirit of a man who is concerned about those of varying backgrounds finding a common ground, but who is concerned, too, with more individual issues such as personal identity and the meaning of home. San Francisco is Laurence Yep's home, by way of a somewhat circuitous family history. His father, Yep Gim Lew, was born in China and joined his own father, a railroad worker in the United States, at the age of ten. Yep's mother, Franche Yep, was born in Lima, Ohio, and reared in Clarksburg, West Virginia, before moving to California, where she met her future husband through their involvement in sports. Their first son is Spike, whose given name is Thomas. Laurence is their only other child.

It was Spike who gave Laurence his name, after "a saint he had been studying in school—a saint that had died a particularly gruesome death by being roasted on a grill like a leg of lamb" (*Lost Garden*, 11). Perhaps this circumstance prefigures Yep's interest in adventure, conflict, and warfare of the sort that is so much a part of the Dragon series. When he and his father flew kites, for instance: "The sparrow kites interested me the most since they were used for duels" (5). He talks about visiting San Francisco's De Young Museum, "which in those days had a marvelous collection of weapons, from small little tankettes . . . to strange spears with three twisting corkscrewlike blades" (19). He talks, too, about his collection of toy soldiers: "In time, I went from individual battles to entire campaigns and even wars; and often the background became as important as the warfare" (79). Very easily, the same statement can be applied to his writing, as will be borne out in following chapters. Just as revealing is the context in which Yep places this discussion about war toys: He created these wars and worlds because, often, he had to rely on his own imagination for diversion and entertainment.

Even more than diversion and entertainment, however, Yep's imagination was a survival mechanism. One of the earliest points in the autobiography where he mentions his imagination is when his neighborhood was going through changes with old residents and friends moving away and housing projects being built. He felt "isolated and alone" as he tried to make sense of the changes: "Had I done something wrong? Was this a punishment? I wound up falling back upon my own imagination, learning to value games that I could play by myself" (*Lost Garden*, 23).

His games with his imagination have become, too, his livelihood. One of the most ironic anecdotes in the autobiography occurs during his college years at Marquette University in Milwaukee, Wisconsin. Majoring in journalism, he was told by one of his professors that he "had more of a talent for fiction than for fact" (*Lost Garden*, 100). A bit disillusioned with his studies and feeling as though he were wasting his parents' modest resources by pursuing his education (though they were completely supportive): "I found myself turning inward. Stuck physically in Milwaukee, I could only go back to San Francisco in my imagination" (101). It was at this point that he wrote his first science fiction story, "The Selchey Kids," for which he was paid a penny a word, and which went on to be included in the *World's Best Science Fiction of 1969* (101). Yep had learned one of the major themes that he explores in *Dragon Steel*: "the mind can go any place it wants."[8]

There are many facets of the mind of the man called Laurence Yep. Speaking about characterization and narrative voice, he explains how he "settles into" whatever character acts as a focus for a book's viewpoint. He goes on to mention the effect that this has on his personal life: "[My wife] particularly disliked it when I was writing about Shimmer the dragon because the 'dragon' in me would also come out" (*Lost Garden*, 106).

In light of his science fiction and fantasy worlds, it comes as no surprise to Yep's fans that there is also a scientist in him; at one point, he was torn between majoring in chemistry and English in college (*Lost Garden*, 92). While contemplating this dilemma, he recalls: "I realized that I enjoyed making stories even more than making bombs. It was more of an impulse at that point in my life; but that is the way many self-truths reveal themselves—like a sprout germinating from a seed that has to work its way up through the dark soil and find a path that will lead it up from underneath a rock" (93). Of course, he became a writer. And the garden imagery in this passage undergirds *The Lost Garden*, Yep's autobiography, which chronicles his development as both an individual and a writer.

The garden of the title refers specifically to his father's garden, and writing the autobiography served as a kind of therapy after his father's death. But other members of his extended family are important as well. When his imagination takes him home to San Francisco from Milwaukee, it is a home populated with his brother, mother, grandparents, nieces, aunts, uncles, and cousins. It is largely based on their stories and histories, in concert with his imagination and his own experience, that he nurtures his "garden of dragons" and his other books. His Dragon series is a major achievement, set as it is in magical worlds. But often, the site of Yep's garden is San Francisco, the place he will always call home: "I couldn't live anywhere else."[9]

Laurence Yep experienced at least two different San Franciscos—inside and outside of Chinatown. He lived outside of Chinatown in an apartment above his parents' grocery store. The hard work and the daily routine of operating the store taught him many things: "[My chores] gave a rhythm to my day to which I became accustomed—a habit which still proves useful" (*Lost Garden*, 21). One of the writers he discusses in the autobiography is Mark Twain, whose experiences inspired *The Tom Sawyer Fires* and *The Mark Twain Murders*. He notes in particular Twain's contention that "he learned everything he needed to know about human nature" aboard the boats he rode up and down the Mississippi River. And making an unexpected but appropriate connection, Yep sees the store as "my version of one of Mark Twain's steamboats, giving me my first schooling as a writer" (28).

In his neighborhood were a few Chinese people (it was not until the relaxation of housing discrimination in the 1960s that Chinese began to move outside of Chinatown in large numbers), a large proportion of black people, some white people, and a few "beatnik filmmakers" (because rents were inexpensive). He attended St. Mary's Grammar School, near Chinatown, which had been a mission to convert Chinese Americans (*Lost Garden*, 52). The older members of his family were not Christians, and the only connection Laurence had with their traditional and sacred New Year celebration was the firecrackers that he was allowed to shoot off. His immediate family did not speak Chinese at home, and so when St. Mary's was transformed from a "regular" school into a Chinese school, Laurence "resented being put into the dummies' class and forced to learn a foreign language" (52).

There are two especially revealing passages in Yep's autobiography. The first incident takes place as he stands on the sidewalk, overseeing groceries that must be taken into the store: "I remember a group of children who came down the block, both black and white. They were pretending they were soldiers in World War II. Suddenly they began making me a target, assuming that I was Japanese. Saul came along and chased them off; but I realized that I was the neighborhood's all-purpose Asian" (*Lost Garden*, 38). The second takes place in his home while he watches a cartoon show in which the protagonist enters into a conflict with Chinese laundrymen. To Yep, these caricatured characters did not seem real, "and I remember putting my fingers up by the sides of my eyes to slant them like the characters in the cartoon and running around making high, sing-song noises. My horrified mother said to me, 'You're Chinese. Stop that'" (41). These passages are fascinating for several reasons. First, they demonstrate how complicated it is for people to work through the issue of ethnic and personal identity. On the one hand, the young Yep is ostracized because he is Asian, though, as in his language class anecdote, he thinks of that which is Chinese as foreign to some extent. Those who taunt him are not educated enough to know, or care, that there are various Asian cultures. On the other hand, he is so much a part of American mainstream culture that he does not readily recognize images, though distorted, of his own ethnic community.

These passages say just as much, however, about American society as they say about Laurence Yep. He recognizes this by putting his own feelings of not wanting to be Chinese into a larger context of the importance of conformity in America of the 1950s and earlier. For example, Harry Truman once wrote to his wife, "I think one man is just as good as another so long as he's honest and decent and not a nigger or a Chinaman." He continued, "[Uncle Will] does hate Chinese and Japs. So do I. It is race prejudice, I guess. But I am strongly of the opinion Negroes ought to be in Africa, yellow men in Asia and white men in Europe and America."[10] Laurence Yep contrasts this kind of attitude to the present, "when so many children are now proud of their ethnic heritages" (*Lost Garden*, 43). His literature, certainly, contributes to the current climate to which he alludes. To Laurence Yep, multiculturalism is an honorable concept—more than a fad, he says, and more like a tide. His willingness to confront what he calls his Chineseness, through his books, helps Chinese- and Asian-American young people confront this issue themselves. Author and critic Maxine Hong Kingston expresses her own enthusiasm about Yep's writing this way: "There are scenes in *Child of the Owl* . . . that will make every Chinese-American child gasp with recognition. 'Hey! That happened to me. I did that. I saw that,' the young reader will say, and be glad that a writer set it down, and feel comforted, less eccentric, less alone."[11] At the same time, Yep's writing has the potential to help non-Asians to understand the issue vicariously. Depending on the specific cast of characters, the identification is direct.[12]

The person who most helped Laurence Yep to confront his Chinese heritage was his maternal grandmother, Marie Lee.

Because she did not speak English, they could not communicate verbally as much as they would have liked. "Instead, what I learned, I picked up in a subtle fashion, soaking up things like a sponge so that years later I was able to use it in a book" (*Lost Garden*, 49). These things included ways of dressing, smells, tastes, and a feel for the "right" way to do things such as the preparation of rice, and most significant, a respect for history and experience. It was largely because of her influence that Yep began when he was still young to keep a file of family stories that he would use later in *Child of the Owl*, which is largely connected to his grandmother's experience; *Sea Glass*, which is his favorite because it is in many ways about his father and uncles; and *Dragonwings*, in which one of the main characters, Windrider, is inspired by the kite-flying of Yep's own father.

This concern is reflected even in his fantasy books. When Shimmer is reunited with a former teacher in *Dragon Steel*, she introduces herself this way: "A very stubborn young dragon once told you that she didn't want to learn history because it was boring. And you told her that history was like a great beast that one either learned how to ride or got trampled by" (*Steel*, 167). It is this same teacher, Lady Francolin, who, even in her old age, is trying to put together an oral history of her clan. Yep's work is a beautiful translation, blending, and transformation of the oral into the written. And just as Yep constructs family histories starting with the stories of individuals, he knows that even larger histories, those of countries and societies, are often best told through the stories of ordinary people.

Laurence Yep, the writer, is and has been always a reader himself. In particular, he enjoyed the fantasy books of Andre Norton, whose appeal for him was "the exotic worlds she created with their mysterious, half-ruined cities" (*Lost Garden*, 78). But more revealing and significant is his response to L. Frank Baum's Oz series: "In the Oz books, you usually have some child taken out of his or her everyday world and taken to a new land where he or she must learn new customs and adjust to new people. There was no time for being stunned or for complaining. The children took in the situation and adapted. . . . The Oz books talked about survival. They dealt with the real mysteries of life—like finding yourself and your place in the world. And that was something I tried to do every day I got on and off the bus" (77).

At this point in his life, Laurence Yep has gotten on and off the bus not only to go to school in Chinatown and then return home, but in many other places over several decades. After studying at Marquette University, he transferred to the University of California at Santa Cruz, where he completed his bachelor's degree in 1970. He earned a doctorate in English from the State University of New York at Buffalo in 1975, where he wrote his dissertation on Faulkner, another writer, as Yep notes, who could not escape his home. Since that time, Yep has been a professor of literature and of creative writing at various universities, including Foothill College in Mountain View, California, San Jose City College in San Jose, California, and the University of California at Berkeley.

And Yep has had great success as a writer. He has been a Book-of-the-Month-Club fellow and he has won the International Reading Association Award, the National Council for the Social Studies Woodson Award, and the Women's International League for Peace and Freedom Jane Addams Award. In addition, he has won numerous prestigious awards in the field of children's and young adult literature. *Dragonwings* garnered enthusiastic recognition, including being named a 1976 Newbery Honor Book. *Child of the Owl* was the winner of the 1977 *Boston Globe–Horn Book* Fiction Award, among other honors. *Dragon of the Lost Sea* was an American Library Association Notable Children's Book of 1982. Along with other distinctions, *The Rainbow People*, a folklore collection, garnered a 1989 *Boston Globe–Horn Book* Honor Award for Nonfiction. His *Dragon's Gate*, dedicated to Charlotte Zolotow, was designated a 1994 Newbery Honor Book.

Zolotow, a well-respected children's book editor, was Laurence Yep's first editor at Harper and Row. Her assistant was Joanne Ryder, Yep's college friend who would become his wife. It was she who showed his work to Zolotow, and his career in the world of children's literature began with the publication of *Sweetwater* in 1973. Zolotow recognized Yep's gift for depicting interpersonal relationships and his sense of humor. Further, she contends that he is one of the most intellectual of American children's authors. She recalls that his manuscripts required little editing on her part or revision on his part; they were submitted in nearly perfect shape. Zolotow felt strongly that Yep would be good at writing realistic work, in addition to science fiction, and encouraged him to write *Dragonwings. Dragon's Gate* was begun during the same period, and the two books are linked with at least one common character and some of the same issues. Zolotow is touched that the book was dedicated to her but is not surprised that it is an award-winning story.[13] The complete list of Yep's work is so extensive that it demands an entire appendix. Part of what is significant, in any case, is that Yep has won recognition and praise for books in several different genres: historical fiction, fantasy, contemporary realism, and folklore. One of his latest books is *American Dragons: Twenty-Five Asian American Voices*, of which he is the editor. Several reviewers were partially critical. Hazel Rochman, for example, notes that not all of the pieces are equally polished, an observation shared by others. But everyone would, I think, agree with Margaret A. Chang that "the collection is valuable for its new voices and for the old ones drawn from hard-to-find sources." She goes on to say that *American Dragons* is "a kaleidoscopic, occasionally brilliant, illumination of the Asian-American experience."[14] This kind of praise attests to Yep's accomplishment as an editor/anthologist, yet another genre to add to his impressive, inclusive list.

Laurence Yep can be called an extraordinary, ordinary person, whose autobiography employs the metaphors of puzzles and gardens to make sense of the memories that are his life. Memories are, he says, "like apple trees" in that they do not always grow "true"; it is possible for one kind of seed to produce a different variety of apple. Yep makes sense of this in a writer's terms, contending that what might be negative for the planter can be positive for an author: "Memories fall like so many seeds into the imagination where they germinate in their own rhythm and timing; and it doesn't matter if they do not grow exactly as the original. In fact, if the harvest is to be special, it's sometimes better if they don't grow 'true'" (*Lost Garden*, 103). The garden of children's literature is richer and more inviting because of the mutations of the seeds planted and nurtured by Laurence Yep. His "Garden of Dragons," along with his many other books, are just as tenacious as the tenacious Chinese vegetable garden still growing where it was planted by his grandparents in West Virginia. They are just as powerful as the memory of his father's garden, which really is not lost at all.

2. Puzzle Pieces of History

Sweetwater

Sweetwater, Laurence Yep's first novel, is a complex tale. It is the story of Tyree Priest, his family, and his people, the Silkies, who co-inhabit the world of Harmony with the Mainlanders, a rival faction of human colonists. The Mainlanders, who landed on Harmony along with the Silkies, have chosen a different lifestyle, and now the two groups are enemies of a sort: "From the very day the colony was founded, my ancestors had never gotten along with the other colonists. My ancestors had been the crews of the starships that had brought the colonists here, and they had never intended to stay; but when their starships broke down, they were stranded. Because of their background and because of pride, they stayed apart from the other colonists."[1] So the Silkies and the Mainlanders are enemies in that they are members of different economic classes. The Silkies were once the servants of the Mainlanders, who now consider themselves superior. Further complicating the scenario are the Argans, the native inhabitants of Harmony, who are a different form of "alien" life altogether, with a unique physical appearance, language, and culture.

Significantly, each group lives in its own segregated neighborhood. Their relationships are complicated and troubled. It is interesting, however, that the "spacemen [Silkies] had more in common with the aliens than with the colonists [Mainlanders], who as a rule stayed away from the spacemen" (*Sweetwater*, 54). There is mention of one "mixed marriage" between a Silkie and a

Mainlander. But because the story is told from the viewpoint of Tyree (a Silkie), the Mainlander ancestry is blamed for making the offspring, Theophilus, go wrong: "[He] would have made a good Silkie if his mainland mother had not spoiled him with her talk of 'progress'" (59). Silkies who are concerned with "progress" in a narrow, materialistic sense call themselves "The Sons of Light."

It is "progress," however, that brought all the humans to Harmony in the first place: "There isn't enough metal or good soil left on Earth to satisfy her needs. Earth could not survive if her colonies did not ship food and ore to her" (*Sweetwater*, 30). Unfortunately, the "progress" of a greedy, capitalist developer of tourist resorts, Satin (so very like "Satan"), is one of the reasons that the Silkies are now being forced to lose their community.

Against this complex backdrop, Tyree's life is full of both adventure and reflection. He gains an appreciation for the art of music through the tutelage and friendship of his secret Argan mentor. He struggles with his community against not only human adversaries but against the forces of nature. He grows into a mature young man, discovering the meaning of family. This is, in its most simple terms, the story, a story whose movement is toward establishing true harmony on Harmony.

It might seem odd at first to discuss *Sweetwater*, a science fiction book, with *The Serpent's Children*, *Mountain Light*, *Dragon's Gate*, and *Dragonwings*, which are all historical fiction (or historical fantasy, as Yep defines *Dragonwings* in the afterword), in one chapter. They all teach readers a great deal about Chinese history and early Chinese-American experience—a "great deal" because most Americans, the primary audience, are so undereducated about this history. In any case, they are grouped together because, as Yep points out, *Sweetwater* is the book that led him to write *Dragonwings*. He says:

> The thing about science fiction is not so much finding a new machine or a new invention, it's actually seeing human beings in a different situation, in a strange situation. . . . Sometimes I think . . . American science fiction gets lost in gadgetry, and it

can be fun, but, the best science fiction writers . . . have solid characters, as well as good, solid scientific background. . . . The thing about science fiction is being able to meet and confront aliens. They used to call them BEMs, or Bug Eyed Monsters— all the monster would do was try to devour you. But I wanted some friendly aliens, aliens that could help you, who'd not necessarily be completely superior in wisdom, but living their own kind of life.

It only occurred to me after [*Sweetwater*] was published that the aliens of the novel, the Argans, are similar in ways to the Chinese in America. Out of *Sweetwater* grew *Dragonwings*, in which I finally confronted my own Chinese-American identity.[2]

Yep makes this same point over and over again in his autobiography: science fiction, while set in other worlds, cannot help being about us, humans, because humans create science fiction. For those who are interested in writing, he makes the point in still another way:

The first advice a beginning writer gets is to write about what you know; but that doesn't mean that the subject has to be in the same form you saw it. My first science-fiction novel, *Sweetwater*, grew out of my memory of our living room in the Pearl Apartments. One day, as the light was rippling over the ceiling the way light reflects from the surface of a pool, I began to imagine what it would be like if the streets outside our apartment had been flooded—along with the rest of San Francisco. (*Lost Garden*, 91–92)

And what Laurence Yep imagined is magical.

Tyree Priest's home world is Harmony, but his ancestors came from Earth. This information helps the reader to identify with the protagonist from the very first sentence. Young adult readers also identify with the issue of parental pressure. Though most of the humans on Harmony have not made it a priority to learn about Earth, [Tyree's] "Pa said that at least his son would remember Earth. He said that in each generation one of us must be able to tell the others about the old Earth ways, and I guess he was right" (*Sweetwater*, 3–4).

But readers know immediately, too, that they are in another world. Tyree explains Harmony's position in the galaxy. And to get even more specific, facing the first page of text is a map of Old Sion, the city that Tyree, his family, and their fellow Silkies are preparing to leave. The story to come is about "how we lost it. Pa says that no one person's responsible, but I figure Pa's just being nice. If I hadn't wanted to play the flute or go mixing with aliens, we wouldn't have had so much trouble. Anyway, I'm going to try to write about what happened during the last few years. And maybe, just maybe, I can save something of what we're losing— for the generations to come on Harmony and for you people back on Earth who don't know what it's like to live on a star colony" (*Sweetwater*, 4).

It is only the most accomplished writers, like Yep, who can introduce a story so skillfully, pulling readers into the narrative, making an immediate identification between them and the characters, introducing them to a different world, and explaining why the story is being told—all at the same time.

There are many intriguing aspects of *Sweetwater*, the most obvious of which is the water, the aquatic environment. The map shows, beneath an overlay of waves, the coastline of Old Sion, which does exist during periods of dry weather. But throughout the course of the book, the setting is under water, an environment to which the Silkies have adapted over the years. Standing in contrast is the location chosen by the Mainlanders, those colonists who retreated to the land when nature's cycles covered their city in water. There is animal life, both intelligent and unintelligent, hostile and neutral. And Yep has created, too, convincing plant life, the varieties of which serve as light, as decoration, as food— "(Of course, the oysters and clams and seaweed weren't exactly like the kinds you find on Earth, but we gave Earth names to their counterparts on Harmony)" (*Sweetwater*, 5).

The names of the characters are much more important. Tyree's people were labeled by other colonists as Silkies after they adapted so well to the flooded city. But absolutely essential is the information that "The Mainlanders meant it as an insult because the mythical Silkies were so ugly on the land, but my ancestors adopted the name with pride because the Silkies were beautiful in their own mysterious sea" (*Sweetwater*, 4–5). As it turns out, this passage is just one early clue to Yep's interest in the power of names. Throughout *Sweetwater*, and throughout his entire body of work, he demonstrates to young readers the social importance of names. Quite directly, he is addressing the old adage, part of the cultural repertoire of countless Americans, that "sticks and stones may break your bones, but names will never hurt you." He shows how names have meaning for individuals, for members of a group, and for those outside of a group as they refer to others.

Yep plays with names a great deal in *Sweetwater*. For instance, the Silkies' schoolteacher is named Erasmus McGuffey, invoking the legacies of the sixteenth-century humanist, scholar, and theologian (Erasmus) and the nineteenth-century educator and editor of the McGuffey readers for schoolchildren (William Holmes McGuffey). The Argans (whose name is suggestive of Aryans), to whom music means so much, have names such as Sebastian, Amadeus, and Handel, invoking the most renowned of European classical musicians. But the "made-up" names of Yep's "friendly aliens" are of utmost importance: "Argans, like some people on Earth, don't believe in giving their true names because that gives the listener power over the person named" (*Sweetwater*, 21). This is not the "demons" versus the Chinese Americans, but it is the Argans, the indigenous inhabitants of Harmony—"the only intelligent race native to Harmony" (16)—in a power struggle with the human colonists. It is revealing to note, too, Tyree's admission that the humans would not have survived the "new world" without the help of the Argans. He credits them with laying "the basis for independence and survival of the spacemen . . . by teaching them how to live off the seashore" (55). He then continues with a significant analysis: "The Argans helped create the Silkies" (55).

What is interesting, startling, and disturbing in terms of intercultural interaction is that those who immigrated to Harmony refer to the Argans as "aliens"! The situation of Harmony is analogous to Native Americans now being second-class citizens in their own homelands. Taking the same concept a little further,

Yep's readers cannot help but reflect that people of color will soon be the "minority majority" in this country.

Names do hurt the Argans. When Tyree and his Argan friend and musical mentor Amadeus argue, in anger Tyree assaults the Argans with the ultimate insult—"a bunch of old spiders"—a slight referring to their ancestry: "They hate to be reminded of their resemblance to their Earth cousins the way humans hate to be reminded that they look like apes" (*Sweetwater*, 18). When Tyree offers to "take back" his words, Amadeus's response is clear and perceptive: "You know you can never do that" (105).

Laurence Yep and his characters take the power of words seriously: words, once voiced, cannot be taken back. But other things can happen to words. They can be burned. They can be banned. They can be forgotten. They can be misinterpreted or abused. Yep is acutely aware of this problem in the world of publishing. In particular, he is concerned about the way that publishers react to Asian-American writing that is written in pidgin, a combination of Chinese and English. He says: "I literally took [some particular] stories around door-to-door to publishers I knew, saying why don't you publish them as picture books. And they just wouldn't do it." Commenting on their reasons, he continues: "Well, you know, it's that . . . awful word, 'They're not accessible,' which means it's not standard English that all little kids can read, which I think is a mistake." He talks about local color writing of nineteenth-century America and how it did not bother people that it was often read aloud and not every word was understandable. Further, he notes that such books written in the vernacular as *Huckleberry Finn* are part of "the canon" and commonly taught in English departments.

In the case of *Sweetwater*, the body of writing left by the Silkies' ancestors is written in an ancient language, Anglic, understood by only the most educated of the modern-day Silkies, who now speak Intergal, their "hybrid" language (*Sweetwater*, 16). These writings contain information about the way they lived and worked. They contain scientific information, of course, about their travels in space. But any writing also contains "cultural information." Because of the importance of the documents, Pa constantly urges Tyree to study Anglic, reminding him that "there's got to be somebody who can read the logbooks in Anglic and understand what our forefathers said. We can't afford to lose any part of our heritage. Now can we?" (14).

We are pointed back to Laurence Yep's own comments about *Sweetwater*. It is now easy to understand how this book led him to *Dragonwings*; thematically, the books are quite similar. Like Chinese laborers in America, humans never intended to stay on Harmony. Like Chinese workers not allowed by American law to bring their wives with them, Argans live in male communities and refer to each other as "uncle," "nephew," and "cousin." Clearly, critic Brian Stableford did not understand this correspondence between the two books when he says that Yep's reference to Amadeus as "the Ultimate Uncle" is saccharin.[3] Of course, he did not have the advantage of reading Yep's autobiography, *The Lost Garden*, in which he says plainly: "In writing about alienated people and aliens in my science fiction, I was writing about myself as a Chinese American" (*Lost Garden*, 104). Tyree is Yep (or the other way around) when, after he runs away from home, he comes to the realization that: "I had just been thinking of myself. If I had to take account of everything I owed the Silkies and of everything they owed me, why, we'd both be the losers. They were my own kind, whether I liked it or not; I could no more leave them than I could leave myself" (*Sweetwater*, 138). The statement speaks for itself.

And "Sweetwater"—the title of the book and the name of an old Anglic Earth hymn—offers these words:

> Come to the sweet water,
> Cool water, well water;
> By the well a cedar bucket,
> Dip the gourd into the water . . .
> Taste the water, cool water,
> Sweet water, promised.
>
> (*Sweetwater*, 180)

The song is important to the story in several ways. First, it alludes to the vision of Tyree's Great-Great-Grandpa in sinking a pump down to the water table below their house, providing their family, even now, with "the only cool, sweet, fresh water for a hundred miles" (*Sweetwater*, 7). The Priests' is the only "well" in the community. The bucket they use to fetch the water is made of cedar, like the bucket in the Anglic hymn.

The second important thing about the song, played late in the story by Tyree, is that he was able to play it only after being taught the music and the musicianship by an Argan. Third, the Silkies use the song as a unifying force only after "someone realized you could sing the old 'Sweetwater' lyrics to the new tune" (*Sweetwater*, 179). It is at this point, finally, that the Silkies are making peace with their history and with their present, for the good of their future. The feeling that Tyree experiences early in the story now has meaning: "And the feeling grew inside me that by combining the musics of Earth and Harmony, I was creating music that would belong particularly to the Silkies: songs that would celebrate all the hard times and the high times of being a Silkie—yes, and maybe I was creating our soul; for it's a grand and yet a frightening thing to be a Silkie" (29–30). And from Laurence Yep's point of view, perhaps, it is sometimes grand and sometimes frightening to be a Chinese American. And thus, with *Sweetwater*, we have the genesis of his phenomenal cycle of novels that explore the stories of his people, beginning in China and continuing in America.

The Serpent's Children and Mountain Light

Laurence Yep is a storyteller. When discussing his picture book *The Man Who Tricked a Ghost*, he talks about how it would work orally. In his novels, he sometimes interweaves story within story within story. In *The Serpent's Children*, it is only one of the stories within the central story that can explain the book's title. Two of the main characters, Foxfire and Cassia, brother and sister, are descendants of a child born of both human and serpent. After telling them the story of this ancestor, their mother says: "you two mustn't fight, because you're of the same serpent blood. All you really have is one another. . . . You may have the clan name of Young, but you'll always be outsiders to them."[4] It is evident immediately that not only will the reader find stories within stories, but circles within circles of groups of people—individuals, families, clans, provinces, nations; the male, the female; the living, the dead. As Yep himself found out while researching the book: "As a people, the Chinese were not the homogeneous whole that I had expected. . . . The people from Kwangtung province, where this story took place, did not fit at all into passive, self-effacing stereotypes" (Serpent's, 276). And as a result, the story of The Serpent's Children was a challenge to Yep himself, and it is undoubtedly a complex, challenging story for the reader.

The first sentence of The Serpent's Children reads, "We had such high hopes when Father marched off to fight the demons" (1)—an attention-getting opening, to say the least. Young readers are involved instantly, wondering who the "demons" are and who "we" are. The answers come quickly. "We" are the farmers in a village "in the Middle Kingdom—or China, as the demons called it" (2). They find out, too, that "these British demons wanted to force the government to let them sell their opium here" (2). Moreover, they have brought slaves along with them. So it is clear that they are a negative force. But what is impressive about Yep's writing is that it is so balanced. Just as he is sensitive to Chinese being stereotyped, he is concerned about the issue of stereotyping in general. Accordingly, he cautions the reader that "demons weren't especially evil, since they could do good things for a person as well as bad" (2).

With this struggle against the English invaders serving as a backdrop, the more immediate action occurs among the Chinese themselves. Cassia refers to the Manchus, currently in power, as barbarians. She adds: "And though my parents did not love the Manchus, they loved the demons even less" (Serpent's, 2). Because Cassia's parents did not love the Manchus, they are engaged actively, when not fighting the British, in "the Work"—a revolutionary effort by "the brotherhood" to drive the Manchus out of the country. And on a more intimate level, there is tension between the Young clan and "the Strangers"—people who had been in the village for more than 300 years, but who were still set apart because they had retained their own language and traditions.

Language and tradition, though, are not the only sources of conflict. Cassia's village of Three Willows is in a constant, generations-old struggle with the neighboring village of the Phoenixes—a struggle based on economics: "Their valley, which was so much wider and greener than ours, gave them larger harvests. As a result, they had the tea money—as bribes were called—to make the officials look the other way when the Phoenixes bullied and terrorized the district" (*Serpent's*, 95). Yep, as always, fits much into a few statements. He gets across the idea that money is related to power. Additionally, he fits cultural information into the narrative in a nonintrusive way; the definition of "tea money" does not interrupt the flow of the scene. This is just a small example, but it introduces the ideas of translation and cross-cultural communication—ideas that are emphasized throughout Yep's works.

The scene, though, that is most likely to remain in the memory of any reader, regardless of age, is that in which members of each group confront each other face to face during a skirmish. Cassia reports: "I can remember seeing his angry face, mouth contorted in a shout, his queue done up in a knot at the back of his head. There was a birthmark on his cheek in the shape of a berry, and it seemed to burn a bright purple. It was the first time I had ever seen one of our ancient enemies, and I remember feeling startled because he didn't have monstrous horns of scales. In fact, he looked like any boy in our own clan" (*Serpent's*, 84–85). No horns, no scales. Just hair and eyes and ears, like the people Cassia knows. And something else—this enemy has emotions, too, just like Cassia and the people in her clan. This passage asks, in fact impels, the reader to realize that there are individual faces and feelings behind every group label.

Yep's insight applies not only to political and ethnic groups, but to gender issues as well. Gender bias is, in fact, a strong concern throughout *The Serpent's Children*. Early in the narrative, Cassia admits that "there were times when I felt like pushing [my brother] down the nearest well. Mother and Father seemed willing to forgive Foxfire more because he was a boy" (*Serpent's*, 3). But Cassia comes to cherish Foxfire; he is the only one to come to her rescue when she is nearly subjected to an extreme form of gender victimization—the binding of feet.

Yep introduces the issue most believably. Like the entirety of the book, this particular episode unfolds convincingly and wonderfully. The reader constantly learns something new about the characters and their lives, whether positive or negative. Yep devotes the better part of two chapters to exploring the issue of footbinding through Cassia's own experience—a much more effective strategy than exploring it through a secondary character.

After Cassia's father has gone off to battle, and after her mother has died, Uncle Windy and Aunt Piety take responsibility for her and Foxfire. Declares Aunt Piety, "She's going to be the little girl I never had." Uncle Windy continues:

> "And anyway, it's time we trimmed your rough edges to bring out your beauty."
>
> Holding on to my pigtails, I backed away from him. "You're not going to trim my hair," I said.
>
> "No"—he smiled secretively—"not your hair. But what I have in mind will help us marry you off easily when the time comes."
>
> I was puzzled by that, but Uncle Windy wouldn't say anything more. (*Serpent's*, 39–40)

Young readers share Cassia's puzzlement. They share her sense of uncertainty and uneasiness as she holds on to her pigtails. Yep's foreshadowing is operative both within and outside of the narrative, for both characters and readers.

The footbinding chapter is successful in several ways. One of its strengths is that it allows the reader to explore the situation from the viewpoints of several characters, characters who represent different social classes. Uncle Windy and Aunt Piety think that they are giving Cassia the ultimate gift by arranging for her to have her feet bound. After all, with bound feet, she will be attractive to a rich man. The footbinder/matchmaker, Aunt Patience, is very proud that she was able to marry off her own daughter, Lily, to such a man. Holding Lily's foot, she points out to Cassia that "It's shaped just like a lotus blossom, delicate and perfect" (*Serpent's*, 43). This statement stands out if for no other reason than that it articulates the aesthetic basis for admiring a bound foot, which is contrasted with the unbound foot that resembles the ugly roots of a tree (42).

Cassia is the one who exposes the unpleasant side of the lotus blossom; because it is painful to bathe it, it reeks of a horrible smell, which people attempt to hide with perfume. But everyone except Foxfire thinks that Cassia is crazy for not wanting this "gift." Other girls from families such as Cassia's—families that cannot afford to have their daughters' feet bound or raise an acceptable dowry—do not understand that Cassia does not dream of a life free from heavy labor. They do not understand that Cassia wants "to be able to go for long walks and to run" (*Serpent's*, 44). She succeeds in resisting the custom.

Here, as throughout his work, Laurence Yep reminds readers of the importance of stories, with Cassia drawing on her family history: "And I wondered what the White Serpent would have done at a time like this. In the first place, she would never have let fools take her away from her home. And she certainly would never have let them try to cripple her. It was time I started to act like one of her children and fight" (*Serpent's*, 53). But even while Cassia draws her strength from a story, she grasps that others draw a clear separation between stories and reality. During a later confrontation with her "fellow" villagers, when they question her ability to fight against the Phoenixes, she feels "the old familiar resentment welling up inside . . . whenever the subject of my sex was brought up." She continues: "It's one thing for a woman to do all sorts of heroics in a story; it's quite another for a girl to practice the martial arts with the boys—and beat them" (99).

Furthermore, it is clear that girls themselves listen to stories that cast girls in subservient roles and internalize them. Consider the following passage, about Peony, whose "mind was full of hairdos and clothes and romance stories" (*Serpent's*, 115):

"But despite all that nonsense that filled her mind (or perhaps because of it), she got along well with the other girls—while I could not. Still, I found I couldn't get too angry with her. It would have been like boxing with a butterfly. And Mother had always made a point of getting along with even the silliest of females.

"I closed my eyes and murmured to myself a sentence I remembered Mother saying: 'We are spiritual sisters with everyone of our sex. We are spiritual sisters. We are spiritual sisters'" (*Serpent's*, 115).

Like *Sweetwater*, this book reveals the multilayered nature of human relationships. Readers see clearly that no matter what time period is in question, similar questions and issues arise— issues that young readers may think exist only in their own society: Which people have the most money? Which group has the most power? Is literacy—knowing how to read and write—related to the quality of life? How are boys expected to behave? Are the expectations different for girls? How are people treated who do not meet group expectations? What is one's responsibility to one's family, one's clan, one's village, one's nation? Do the answers to these questions depend on specific circumstances of time or place or other details?

Yep, through Cassia, makes it clear, too, that so many of the expectations people have are communicated and continued through stories. And just as there are different kinds of people and relationships, there are different kinds of stories: Cassia draws strength from her family story, but when things seem too good to be true, "It's like being in a fairy tale" (*Serpent's*, 243). The implication here, of course, is that people must recognize separations between fantasy and reality. But always, story is powerful.

It is the story of the Golden Mountain, America, that changes the course of history for many in Cassia's village, and all of those families whose descendants go on to become Chinese Americans. The story holds a special appeal for Foxfire because "there's a golden mountain in the serpent story" (*Serpent's*, 123). Thus Yep tells us too that stories collide, mesh, blur, and complement each other—a foreshadowing, no doubt, of stories and histories to come. One of Cassia's father's last thoughts in the book is this: "No, I'm too old to change my habits. But I'm beginning to suspect that it's a time for the Foxfires and Cassias of this world. . . .

It's an age for new dreams and for people who aren't afraid to make those dreams come true. . . . It's an age for serpent children."

Cassia, with her arm around her father, adds: "Or maybe it's old seed growing in new earth" (274).

The ending of *The Serpent's Children* creates a space for its companion book, *Mountain Light*. This is a book, too, that has its genesis in Yep's family stories. In order to make sense out of all his family memories, Laurence Yep kept a file of family history. It was years after beginning the file, he says, "that I began to understand just how difficult a journey it had been for my grandmother from China, through Ohio and West Virginia and finally to her little home in Chinatown." And as it turns out, to the delight of Yep's fans, the character of Cassia Young is Yep "trying to imagine my grandmother as a teenager and a new bride" (*Lost Garden*, 54).

And indeed, part of the magic of *Mountain Light* for teenagers is that it includes among its several subplots a love story between Cassia and Squeaky. He is, surprisingly, a young man whose face is familiar to Cassia because she once faced him as her village of Three Willows fought his village of the Phoenixes. So there is a message, clearly, about forgiveness and understanding and group loyalty.

Through Squeaky's consciousness and voice, Yep communicates much valuable insight about human behavior. In this book, none of the struggles seen in the last have been resolved: there is still strife between various factions across the whole of China. When one character second-guesses people from a group other than his own, Squeaky explains some of the discord: "They're not always that bad. . . . They're just afraid, but they can't take it out on the ones they're afraid of—the Manchus. So they pick on a target they can reach."[5] With the Manchus still in power, the brotherhood is still active. Thus, one of the major "messages" of the book is an echo from *The Serpent's Children*. Cassia's father, a freedom fighter called the Gallant, reminds her and her comrades before his death of the Brotherhood's motto: Banish the Darkness. Restore the Light. "I think that the Light has to be more than a symbolic name. It's the Light within each of us, and that Light is more important than our own prejudices. We have to live the light. We have to be it" (*Mountain*, 8). These are words that Squeaky, Cassia, and Foxfire will certainly need to keep in mind when this portion of Yep's chronicle of their lives ends with Foxfire and Squeaky in the Land of the Golden Mountain and Cassia waiting at home. The final words of the book are Squeaky's: "Well, . . . whatever happens, we'll make the best of it. As your sister would say, we don't have much choice" (281). Both statements taken together, the lyrical and the practical, serve all of Laurence Yep's characters well.

Dragon's Gate

"When we were at Cape Horn," a wispy little voice said, "Kilroy didn't even try to ask his western crews." The voice sounded raspy, as if it had not been used in a long time. We all turned to see; it was Shaky. His head nodded up and down constantly as he spoke the only words I had ever heard from him. "He came to my crew. We were all young and fresh off the boat. What did we know?" He looked around the cabin. "We wound up dangling over a cliff in a basket, swaying on a rope while we hammered away with a chisel, with only the basket bottoms between us and a fall into forever. And sometimes after we packed the holes and lit the fuses, the fuses were too short or the crew took too long to haul us up. We were lucky if there was enough to bury. Even when the rest of my crew was dead, he kept ordering me to go over. Remember. Someone please remember."[6]

This quotation is from one of Laurence Yep's recently published novels, *Dragon's Gate*. But though it is recent, it is also one of the earliest, begun more than 20 years ago, at the same time as he began *Dragonwings*. At least in part, it has to be Yep's great respect for the very idea of history that gave him the inspiration and diligence to work on such a protracted project. The extensive research it required is articulated clearly in the book's afterword, though it would be evident even without any mention. Thorough research and meticulous documentation are what make it possible for Yep to remember, for him to answer the fictional Shaky's plea that someone remember the experiences of Chinese railroad laborers in America.

Shaky's rare utterance follows a scene in which the Chinese workers gain information about their status and work conditions in contrast to those of white workers. Chinese workers, for example, earned thirty dollars a month compared with the thirty-five earned by white workers. Chinese workers paid for their own food, while food was provided free of charge to white workers. The rules about the length of a shift were honored for white workers but not for Chinese. The list goes on.

The conversation sparked by Shaky's statement is all about history. One character, Bright Star, is adamant that Western history books will proclaim that the white workers alone were the heroes of the railroads. In addition, he suggests indirectly that the Chinese in America occupy a unique, still undefined place—no longer Chinese, but not yet "Chinese Americans"; he contends that Chinese historians "won't care a thread what happens in this barbaric land" (*Gate*, 248). And he warns, "If you keep silent, then you lose by default" (249). His ultimate advice is to do what can be done in the present, regardless of what will be recorded eventually in history books. Laurence Yep is not a historian in the narrow sense of the word. But his historical fiction is the raising of his voice, his refusal to "lose by default" to the sensibilities and biases of Western historians and storytellers.

The framing of *Dragon's Gate* as a historical fiction begins with a preface, impressive for its scope. It addresses current events in both the United States and China, and it goes on to break down those events onto regional as well as national levels. Later in the book, the international problem of colonialism is addressed, too: "You don't hear the news of the world like we do. The European countries are planning to carve up the Middle Kingdom. Britain and Portugal have already grabbed land. Russia's taking land from the north, and England and France are taking land from the south. They'll cut the Kingdom up into separate European colonies. '. . . Just like Africa,' Father said, and went on to describe how the European powers were divvying up that

continent" (*Gate*, 21–22). The preface outlines the recent events
in China at the time the book is set, the summer of 1865. These
events include two significant rebellions against the Manchu
rulers of China. The resulting nationwide unrest results in a
large number of Chinese men departing for America. At this time
in America, one of the momentous national efforts, under the
guidance of President Abraham Lincoln, is to build a transconti-
nental railroad. "By February 1865, the railroad is so desperate
that it has begun experimenting with using Chinese crews"
(*Gate*, preface).

The word "desperate" is an interesting choice. It is meaningful
for what it does not reveal overtly. It challenges young readers to
discover its significance. It closes a paragraph that begins: "By
the summer of 1865, the North has finally defeated the South in
the Civil War, and America works for even greater union" (*Gate*,
preface). Why is it a desperate act to add Chinese workers to a
social situation characterized already by discord? What are the
factions involved? *Who* are Americans? Clearly, the British opium
trade in China is not divorced from European colonialism in
Africa which in turn is not divorced from slavery in America.

It is plain in the narrative that some of those who live in
America are slaves. Otter, the 14-year-old narrator of the story, is
curious, naturally, and disturbed when he first learns this information. When he asks why America has been engaged in a civil
war, his father explains that there are numerous reasons, among
them the freeing of the slaves. Otter thinks:

> Nothing I heard about *America* should have seemed strange by
> now; but it did anyway. All my life I had been taught that if
> you're born poor or even a slave, you must have done something
> bad in your previous life. If you do something good, then you're
> rewarded by being born rich in the next. *"But it's fate if you're
> born a slave."*
> Father glanced at Uncle for help, and Uncle plucked at his
> lip as he tried to find the right words in English. *"Everybody
> there, they free. Everybody, they equal."* (*Gate*, 33)

This passage raises several issues. One them is, of course,
cross-cultural understandings and misunderstandings that come

from various cultures' many ways of making sense of their worlds. More specifically, the question at issue is economic class and social status. And underlying all is the idea of freedom.

Otter's preoccupation with class issues begins during his early years in Three Willows Village, Toishan County, Kwangtung Province, China, the setting for the first part of *Dragon's Gate*. As the book opens, Otter's father (Squeaky) and Foxfire, Otter's uncle, are returning from America amid much village fanfare—as "Guests of the Golden Mountain" they have been able to earn money and send it back to their home village to be used not only by their immediate families but by the entire community. Otter, sitting in class, hears the excitement and asks his teacher, Uncle Blacky, to be excused. When Uncle Blacky grants him permission to leave, Otter tells the reader: "What else was he going to say? Most of the subscription for his new school had come from my own family" (*Gate*, 2). This may, in fact, be true, but Otter's attitude, if not arrogant, at least expresses a belief that this is just the way society is set up.

In fairness to Otter, it is critical to acknowledge his own struggle with class status and its consequences for people's lives. He sees, for example, that the schoolmaster treats poor students much more harshly than he treats the rich boys. When Uncle Blacky, frustrated with Otter's insolence, punishes a poor boy, Otter does try to take the blame. When he sees the other poor boys cringing as Stumpy is hit across his palms, Otter wonders to himself:

> What do you do when your family is so powerful that you lead a charmed life and even your teacher won't find fault with you? I tried to bring candy treats on different occasions for all my classmates. The poorer boys were lucky to get a bite of meat in an entire year, let alone taste sugar. And of course, on festivals, I used my allowance to buy toys and firecrackers for everyone. So I don't think they held it against me that Uncle Blacky treated me as his pet. The other guests' sons led just as protected a life. (*Gate*, 3–4)

In the course of the story, however, he does learn that positive interaction between people of different social classes cannot hinge simply on the poor holding or not holding it against the rich that they are privileged. He learns that part of what makes civilized human contact possible is the privileged also taking responsibility not only for their attitudes, but for their actions as well.

Otter comes to think through some of these issues partly by learning from his parents. Otter's adoptive mother is none other than Cassia of *The Serpent's Children* and *Mountain Light*. As readers would expect, in addition to teaching Otter the formal family history, she makes it a point to tell him countless times: "The astrologers say you were born in the hour of fire on the day of fire in the month of fire, so you were born to join my family, because we've been rebels and troublemakers for seven generations" (*Gate*, 5). For Cassia, part of being a rebel, in addition to fighting political causes on a national stage, is her resolve to live her everyday life the way she wants to live it. She marries Squeaky, a Lau from Phoenix Village, at a time when intermarriage between the two clans was considered totally unacceptable. Adding to what Otter calls her "weirdness" (12), Cassia decided to remain in her own family's village rather than to move to her new husband's village. Now, as the wife of a wealthy and respected man, she still works in her fields, wears modest clothes, and behaves civilly. She does not have a maid, as does her sister-in-law, who "thought having Muslim servants from the north gave her household a kind of exotic elegance" (24). Cassia walks rather than allow herself to be carried in a sedan chair. "As the clan said, Mother still had mud between her toes" (4).

Just as relevant is Otter's observation that "despite his wealth and reputation, Father had just as much mud between his toes as mother, which made them a good match" (*Gate*, 11). Something else makes them a good match: they have their own ideas about male and female roles—ideas that are not traditional. For example, Squeaky credits much of the family's financial security to Cassia's skills in managing money (10). And in other ways, too, she has an equal say in making decisions for the family. She makes it clear to Squeaky, for instance, that she knows what he communicates to their son, even from America: "Anything that comes into this house gets read to me" (29). When Otter approaches his father about returning to America with him, the father's reply is that "I couldn't take you without [Cassia's] permission" (26). And when Uncle Foxfire, Squeaky, Cassia, and Otter all discuss the possibility of Otter's going to America with his uncle and father, "[Father] was too afraid of Mother to say anything" (34). Cassia's final words in this scene are: "I won't have any more talk about that cursed land. It's bad enough you two keep walking in the clouds. My boy's feet stay firmly on the ground" (36). Herein lies one of the central conflicts of the book. At issue is not only the tension between the dreamers and the realists, but the contradictions and disparities between myths and reality.

The myths that Yep explores most thoroughly in *Dragon's Gate* are myths about America. One of the strongest, again, has to do with social class. Though Otter expresses his belief that slaves are fated to be slaves, it seems that this belief is one that he associates primarily with Chinese culture. But part of his desire to go to America is based on his belief that one is in some measure divorced from fate or family history: "At times like these, I yearned to go someplace where it wouldn't matter what my birth parents had been. Someplace like the Golden Mountain" (*Gate*, 14).

What are "times like these"? They are the times when Otter is ridiculed because or reminded that his birth parents, Tiny and Aster, are Strangers. Their status is explored in the two earlier books, and in *Dragon's Gate*, a generation later, they are still outcasts. The general disdain for them is manifested in big ways such as massacres, but also in everyday ways, such as in the games children play: "In the lane some smaller children were playing a game of Hunt the Stranger and were arguing about who was going to be the dirty, stinking, greedy Stranger whom the others would hunt. Though it made me want to shiver, I hid my feelings as I always did when someone spoke of Strangers" (*Gate*, 12). This is just one example of the genius of Laurence Yep. The books some people describe so patly as historical fiction are much more: they show the concrete impact of the abstract concept of history on the real course of events for continents, countries, regions, communities, and individuals. Children's games, as much as any cultural artifact or activity, reveal attitudes that are entrenched in any given society. The games children play expose prejudices, dreams, and mythologies. The same is true of the expressions that work their way into languages. In the region in which Otter lives, one common expression is "as dumb as a Stranger" (43).

Really masterful is how Yep uses the character of Otter to explore the issue of class. Otter embodies all the contradictions, all the inconsistencies, all the tensions of any class-bound society. Though he feels the pain of belonging, at least biologically, to a despised class of people, it is still within him to treat other people condescendingly. What makes this possible, of course, is the status he enjoys because of who his adoptive parents are. A striking, pivotal incident of this occurs after his father and uncle have gone back to America, leaving him to be a "country gentleman" and run the family businesses. During the beautiful early winter season, Otter decides to visit Dragon's Gate, where "ages ago, someone had erected a stone gate that stood astride the river just as it thundered out of a deep gorge and then thundered swiftly down the mountainside. It's said that if a fish can make the long, difficult swim upstream and through the gate, it will change into a dragon. If you want to wish good luck to someone sitting for the government exams, you give that person a picture of a fish swimming through the Dragon's Gate" (*Gate*, 39).

While sitting in a restaurant that has a good view of the Gate, Otter becomes irritated because he is sitting close to a person whom he perceives to be merely a lowly drunkard. Instead of leaving the restaurant, Otter decides to ask the man to stop singing. His decision to do this is based, at least in part, on his attitude that he is entitled to make the request because he is "the son of a prominent, wealthy house" (*Gate*, 41). As it turns out, the man is a Manchu, a mortal enemy of the Rebel forces, for whom Otter's parents have fought so diligently all their lives. As a result of the ensuing confrontation and fight, the Manchu ends up dead. When the Manchus, inevitably, blame Otter for what has happened, his life is in danger, and it is then that he makes the journey to America. So though Otter is fascinated and even preoccupied with the notion of equality, it is his own arrogance, based on notions of superiority and inferiority, that changes the course of his life and situates him in the Land of the Free in January 1867.

In one of the last conversations that Otter has with his mother, they talk about his identity. As the adopted Stranger son of a Rebel couple, he is, Cassia concludes, "neither horse nor water buffalo, neither Stranger nor Young" (*Gate*, 48). This is a fitting send-off to America because it anticipates all of the questions about identity that are raised by the very idea of the country called America. Otter will find out not only why certain people think of it as a desperate act to work alongside Chinese workers but that it is not just him, but America and Americans who are looking for identity. Through another conversation, on the other side of the Pacific Ocean, Otter begins to deal with the issue of status, but in a new context.

The first westerner Otter meets is a boy about Otter's own age, but with a face "covered with brown spots," "green eyes instead of a normal brown, and his hair was as red as fire" (*Gate*, 64). When the boy discusses with Otter the food they have been served, Otter's response is: "I wasn't used to having a stranger discuss my digestion. In the Middle Kingdom, no one would have dared. It made me realize that I was not only exploring a strange new land, but meeting a new people as well. What status did I have with the westerners now?" (67). As the two of them, Otter and Sean, continue to interact, Sean offers some advice to Otter about how to protect himself from the severe winter weather in the Sierra Mountains, where they will be working on the railroads. When he sees that Otter is "surprised to find such sympathy," he explains that he is able to pass on advice only because he, too, has been in the same position: "And weren't we all newcomers to the mountains once?" (67). So Sean forces Otter to consider the fact that America is, indeed, a nation of immigrants.

Another truth that Otter must confront is that once the immigrants are in America, they do not leave behind all of the struggles they confronted in their homes of origin. He finds out as soon as he reaches the work site that the Chinese workers are divided into crews based largely on their home regions in China. "Even Shifty had been dispatched to a crew of Strangers—each to his own kind" (*Gate*, 81). There is tension between some of the workers and those, like Otter, whom they label "one of those spoiled little princes back in China living off his Daddy's money" (100). But in the end, it is Squeaky, Otter's "mud between the toes" father, who articulates the ways in which regional or other kinds of groupings are not useful or cohesive forces, but entirely negative. He decries that "we call ourselves children of the T'ang . . . but we don't act like it. . . . Everyone thinks of his family first, and then his clan, and maybe his home district. But that's it. That's how the Manchus stay in power, because they play us off against one another. And that's how the westerners control us" (189). The ultimate traitor, of course, is the Chinese man (in this case, Shrimp) who, in effect, works as an overseer for the white man because of his own individualistic reasons—a situation reminiscent of the "Uncle Tom" in American slave society.

Freedom, slavery, and equality are Otter's preoccupations throughout the novel. This is especially so when he realizes that his father and uncle do not enjoy the status in America that they had in China. Foxfire tells him forthrightly, "I'm not the boss here" (*Gate*, 92). He adds, "In the Middle Kingdom, I'm somebody; but here I'm just one more worker" (93). Finally, he advises: "Get it through your head, boy, or you won't live out a day. In the Middle Kingdom, you and I were on the top of the heap, but here we're on the bottom. Question the bosses or talk back, and they'll kill you in a dozen different ways" (93). When Otter responds by pointing out that it was from them that he learned that "everyone was free and equal in *America*," his father "spread his arms in exasperation. . . . 'They're better in theory than in practice'" (94).

One of the hopeful aspects of *Dragon's Gate* is that Otter and Sean represent a new generation of Americans who strive to reconcile the dream with the reality. But dreams are not realized without tension and struggle. Though Otter is appalled at first that Sean would speak to him about his digestion, Otter also finds that "Sean had no sense of status, which gave him an open-mindedness that I found refreshing" (*Gate*, 127). And at the most optimistic moments, Otter feels that "[we] had founded our own country with just two citizens; and it didn't matter what the westerners or T'ang people thought" (134). There is at least one moment, too, when both of them sense that there are always going to be some points of intercultural misunderstanding—some things that the other will not be able to make sense of because of their different ways of understanding the world and the behavior of people.

Neither Yep nor Otter dwells on this, though. What they concentrate on is what and who the new Americans will be. Otter realizes that as a teenager—as young as that is or as old as that is—he does not understand all aspects of even Chinese culture (*Gate*, 130). Still, he must forge an identity based not only on being both Young and Stranger, but on being both Chinese and American—someone whom his father and uncle would call "a true guest." As they tell him: "You can never go home now. When you go to Three Willows, you'll see things with western eyes. . . . Once you guest on the Golden Mountain, you change inside" (197). Put most eloquently: "Uncle Foxfire said guesting here had given him a double set of eyes" (238). Without this double set of eyes, survival is not possible.

And perhaps survival is what this story is about, this story that is in some ways the ultimate adventure story. Chinese boy immigrates to the young country of America, striving to fulfill the expectations of the family and community at home as well as his own dreams. Boy, father, and uncle work hard, fighting against the forces of nature and technology and a foreign people and culture. Young readers will be absorbed by the story, which is written with so much detail, passion, and insight that the voices of characters can be heard, the cold in the mountains can be felt, and the loneliness and bravery of trying to forge a new life is tangible. Readers share Otter's sense of satisfaction when he feels, at last, that he has reached a milestone in his life, that he "[has] passed through [his] own Dragon's Gate" (*Gate*, 262), and that he realizes the real significance of coming to America (267).

Dragonwings

Dragonwings is set in San Francisco between 1903 and 1910. Read as a memoir, it is the story of Moon Shadow, who immigrates there to join his father, leaving behind his mother and other extended family members in China. He confesses in the very first sentence: "Ever since I can remember, I had wanted to know about the Land of the Golden Mountain, but my mother had never wanted to talk about it."[7] This opening paragraph ends with the astonishing information that "Moon Shadow's own grandfather had been lynched about thirty years before by a mob of white demons almost the moment he had set foot on their shores" (*Dragonwings*, 1).

Much is embedded in this first paragraph. First, there is the idea of talking and passing on stories and information. Not only did Moon Shadow's mother not *want* to talk about America; she would not. As he tells the reader, "Mother usually said she was too busy to answer my questions" (*Dragonwings*, 2). There are many reasons for her silence, including her own ignorance about America, since she had never been there herself. On the other hand, it is her limited but meaningful knowledge and her insight about the complexities of this place called America that keep her from talking. Perhaps her silence is meant, in some small way, to allow Moon Shadow to retain his idealism about the Golden Mountain and the promise that it represents to the many immigrants who make up its population.

Despite his mother's silence, Moon Shadow hears stories from others. And what comes across in this first paragraph, too, is that each and every word in a story is important. A phrase that jumps out at readers is "white demons," a description that makes sense in the context of a mob committing violence against a man simply because he is of a certain national origin. But the narrator is defining all white people as demons, and the mob is just a subset of them. Later in the first chapter, Moon Shadow elaborates: "Perhaps I should explain here that the T'ang word for demon can mean many kinds of supernatural beings. A demon can be the ghost of a dead person, but he can also be a supernatural creature

who can use his great powers for good as well as for evil, just like
the dragons. It is much trickier to deal with a demon of the Middle
Kingdom than an *American devil*, because you always know that
the *American devil* means you harm" (*Dragonwings*, 10). But even
as it clarifies, this passages brings complexities to the foreground.
No, all demons are not evil. But yes, all American devils are evil.

Clearly, one of the issues in question here is stereotyping. In an
essay entitled "Writing Dragonwings" (see appendix 2) Yep discusses his difficulty in researching Chinese-American history and
the further difficulty of seeing Asian Americans as individuals
rather than stereotypes. Some of the common stereotypes from
popular American culture include the "pompously wise" Charlie
Chan, the "loveable" house boy Peter in *Bachelor Father*, the
"stoic" Cain of *Kung Fu*, and the "cruel and cunning Fu Man
Chu."[8] So part of Yep's "project" with *Dragonwings* is to create
some well-rounded characters to stand alongside, if not replace,
some existing stereotypes.

Moon Shadow, whose voice the reader hears first, has feelings,
preconceptions, and stereotypes of his own. Thus, at the same
time that white readers might feel a bit disturbed by the use of
the phrase "white demon" they must also acknowledge that Yep,
as the narrator, is showing favoritism to no character, to no specific community of people.

One particular passage of Yep's autobiography is especially useful in understanding this facet of him as a writer. He describes
wanting to incorporate into a story a teacher with whom he did
not get along. His intention was "to show how mean she was."
He goes on to describe how in order not to create merely a "card-
board cartoon," the writer must try to understand things from
the perspective of the character. So as he wrote he began to
understand the teacher's attitude toward him and how she
(mis)interpreted his behavior. The "moral of the story" is, in
Yep's words, that "writing is always a kind of balance" (*Lost
Garden*, 54). This balance is communicated to the reader from
the very first paragraph of the book. Moon Shadow might be
biased in certain ways, but Yep never is. It is crucial that readers
make the distinction.

Of course, the issue of stereotyping infuses Laurence Yep's canon, whether set in the Middle Kingdom or on Harmony or in America. But its treatment is especially interesting in *Dragonwings* because of the particular cast of characters and their interactions and relationships. Not only is there interaction within the Chinese bachelor community in Chinatown, there is the interaction between Moon Shadow, his father, and the white American community. It is significant, too, that this interaction crosses lines not only of ethnicity, but of socioeconomic class, age, religion, and gender as well.

One thing that is fascinating about stereotype is that often it is rooted partially in reality. For instance, people frequently think of Chinese Americans as laundry workers. The truth is that many laundries were, in fact, run by Chinese Americans, not because they had any special expertise, but because they were relegated, in this society, to service industries and servile positions. Likewise, there are those white characters who fit Moon Shadow's stereotype of the American demon. Walking through a neighborhood outside of Chinatown, he sees and hears a group of boys calling out:

> Ching Chong Chinaman,
> Sitting in a tree,
> Wanted to pick a berry
> But sat on a bee.
>
> (*Dragonwings*, 118)

The taunts are accompanied by physical abuse. Other examples, more serious examples, occur in the story.

Consistent with the balance characteristic of Yep's writing, though, there are passages such as the following, which describes Moon Shadow's preconceptions about what a white lady would look like: "She was the first demoness that I had ever seen this close up, and I stared. I had expected her to be ten feet tall with blue skin and to have a face covered with warts and ear lobes that hung all the way down to her knees so that her ear lobes would bounce off the knees when she walked. And she might have a potbelly shiny as a mirror, and big sacs of flesh for breasts, and maybe she would only be wearing a loin cloth" (*Dragonwings*, 101). This description is outrageous and funny. But embedded in it are real fears. The image of the loincloth, in particular, implies some level of barbarity, a lack of "civilized" behavior—a trait that many people assign to any foreigners. But what follows is a description of Miss Whitlaw's actual appearance, kindly and calming, and Moon Shadow's immediate reaction: "There were demons, after all, who could be kindly disposed" (101).

Even more notable, perhaps, are the realizations that Moon Shadow expresses later. It is this demon, after all, who helps him to learn English. And it is she and her niece with whom Moon Shadow and his Chinese extended family experience the San Francisco earthquake of 1906. "Another thing to say for the demoness was her genuine interest in learning about people as people. Where some idiot like myself would have been smug and patronizing, the demoness really wanted to learn. And like Father, she was not afraid to talk to me like an equal. '*I don't think I understand*'" (116). This passage occurs during a conversation about the nature of dragons. And thematically, it harkens back to earlier passages about demons. What they both suggest is that different individuals, as well as different peoples, have distinct ways of experiencing the world. Some have ongoing interaction with a supernatural world. Some do not. Some function in extended families. Some do not. And so forth.

Part of the interest young readers have in Yep's work is generated by his attention to the intriguing differences and/or similarities between Eastern and Western cultures. Moon Shadow compares writing systems: "Since the words of the Tang people were more alive—more like pictures, really—handwriting was more of an art form than among demons" (*Dragonwings*, 22). He compares calendars (59). He comments several times on the difference between how Chinese and westerners calculate a person's age (5). He even points out that West and East are relative terms.

Speaking of the West: "(to me it was east, though, since I judged things geographically in relation to the Middle Kingdom)" (127). In a fight with white American boys, Moon Shadow also comes to recognize some of the things that people of different cultures might share: "[Jack] held out his bloody hand. I took it and helped pull him up. Suddenly I realized that these demons were like the Tang boys I knew at home. You only had to punch out the biggest and toughest of the bunch and the others would accept you. Well, Jack was the biggest and toughest of his group. He looked down at me. 'Say, you know, you're all right, Chinaboy,' he said" (*Dragonwings*, 145).

Another example comes from Windrider, Moon Shadow's father, after he repairs the vehicle of a white man: "We might not be able to speak too well with the demons, but in machines there's a language common to us all. You don't have to worry about your accent when you're talking about numbers and diagrams" (*Dragonwings*, 58).

These passages speak for themselves. But people cannot speak for themselves under all circumstances. For as Windrider points out, there are various languages and kinds of languages. And it both startles and intrigues many of Yep's readers when they first realize that in his books with Chinese characters (distinct from Chinese American), the text in italics represents English; Chinese is the norm, and English is the "foreign" language. At the very least, this forces young readers to reconsider some of the assumptions about society and about the world that they might take for granted. More specifically, they are forced to realize that their experiences are not always shared experiences or the reference point for a nonexistent universal experience. In short, they must confront their ethnocentrism.

Certainly, though, it is essential that Moon Shadow learn to communicate in English. In fact, part of the reason that his father decides he should come to the Golden Mountain at the age of eight is, as Hand Clap, a member of his father's extended household, articulates, "He'll learn the demon tongue better when he's young" (*Dragonwings*, 9). After he actually arrives in America, "All during the day, Uncle and Father would keep up a conversation with me using what they knew of the demons' tongue, and they made me read and discuss the demons' magazines and newspapers which some of our friends and kinsmen, who worked in the demons' mansions, would bring down to us" (50). Part of why it is imperative that Moon Shadow master English is that, in part, language is the ticket to his acquiring the "American Dream." And what the preceding passage suggests is that acquiring a language entails more than being able to give a literal translation. One must also understand the attitudes, living circumstances, civic life, and intellectual life of the speakers of a given language; hence, the magazines and newspapers. Translation must go a step further and involve interpretation. And sometimes translation and interpretation must be stretched to include the act of "becoming." In *Dragonwings*, this becoming, this transformation, is, to a certain degree, from Chinese to Chinese American.

In a funny way, too, this acculturation is completely consistent with Chinese thought. Consider this passage:

> As Father led me up the stairs, I forgot about the demons, for I began to wonder again about his name, Windrider. Every Tang man can have several names. He has a family and a personal name given to him at birth. He can have another name given to him when he comes of age, a nickname from his friends, and if he is a poet, he can have a pen name. We are not like demons, who can lock a child into one name from birth—with maybe a nickname if he is lucky. We feel that a man should be able to change his name as he changes, the way a hermit crab can throw away his shell when it's too small and find another one. (*Dragonwings*, 32)

This is a beautifully written passage, encompassing several ideas at once. One of these raises questions about the individual in relationship to the group. Yet another is the idea that the artist holds a special place in society, worthy of a special name. The comparison with the "demon" naming system raises the issue of not only cultural difference, but of intercultural misunderstanding and tension. And finally, there is the crucial notion of change, which comes up throughout Yep's canon.

This is a key passage because, ultimately, as much as it is about Moon Shadow negotiating a new culture, *Dragonwings* is about his building a relationship with his father, and the father reaching for his own dream—a dream intimately bound with his name, Windrider.

Several characters in *Dragonwings* have dreams. But not all of these characters have been able to act upon their dreams. Some may not have acknowledged their dreams consciously at all. Uncle Bright Star belongs in that category. In *Dragon's Gate*, he is a crotchety old man whom the reader probably does not imagine even having dreams. In *Dragonwings*, the reader is made to realize that people often lack the luxury of pursuing dreams, at least on a grand scale. A large portion of Uncle Bright Star's life is spent laboring on the American railroads, where he has injured himself irreparably. But upon meeting Moon Shadow he bestows the gift of a carving of Monkey, a creature with mythical significance to the Tang people. Moon Shadow responds to the gift: "The object that he had treated so casually was beautifully meticulous. It was a work of art. In a better time and place, Uncle might have been a sculptor. It was only later that I saw how rheumatic Uncle's hands were, when he could sometimes barely grip his chopsticks. I realized then just how much effort it must have taken for him to hold a knife and wield it so painstakingly. It was more than a work of art. It was a work of love" (*Dragonwings*, 48). Uncle's dream is manifested in a small but meaningful way. Windrider, in contrast, does not think that pursuing his dream is a luxury. His dream of flying is, to him, essential; it is life-sustaining. It is his past life, his present reality, and he thinks at one point, the future—his total being.

Laurence Yep's books, certainly, represent a coming together of past, present, and future family history: "My father, the kitemaker, became Windrider in *Dragonwings*. . . . Writing *Dragonwings* was a way of stepping into his shoes" (*Lost Garden*, 92). The father-son relationship is important, then, in both fact and fiction. And interestingly enough, it is a story within the larger story of *Dragonwings* that cements the relationship between Windrider and Moon Shadow. After hearing his father's story about his former life as a dragon, "[Moon Shadow] felt as if here at last in the city of the demons, [he] had found [his] true father, and more—a friend and a guide" (*Dragonwings*, 47).

This trust is all the more meaningful because others in the Brotherhood Company of the Peach Orchard Vow, the men with whom they live in San Francisco, believe that Windrider's story— his memory—is merely a dream. And logically, their reaction makes sense because his story is about his life as a dragon—a former life in which he was "the greatest physician of all the dragons, and . . . something of a show-off when it came to flying" (*Dragonwings*, 38). In his "softskin" life this translates into being a master mechanic and kite flyer—a kite flyer living at the same time as the famous Wright brothers and sharing their passion.

The Wright brothers are not the only historical figures who have a presence in *Dragonwings*. During the initial six years of Laurence Yep's research on Chinese-American history: "One of the few early Chinese-Americans in my notes to have a name was Fung Joe Guey who flew a biplane of his own construction over in Oakland in 1909. The scene of his flight seemed so vivid to me that it was easy to put it on paper, but trying to explain how he got to that field with his biplane was difficult" ("Writing," 361). The explanation—*Dragonwings*—is engaging, eloquent, and magical, inspiring for anyone who has ever had a dream. It is because of these qualities that *Dragonwings* is such an honored book, its recognitions including a 1976 Newbery Honor Award and the 1975 International Reading Association Children's Book Award.

The wings, the ability to fly, belong not only to Fung Joe Guey or Windrider or the Wright brothers, but to Laurence Yep as well. Though *Sweetwater* was his first novel for young adults, *Dragonwings* was the book that gave wings to Yep's career in the world of children's and young adult literature. And the story itself continues to fly, now enjoying a resurgence of popularity and exposure as a play, which has toured all over the country.

One of the ideas from the book that is reiterated more than once in the stage production has to do with "the stranger." This term is used differently in *Dragonwings* than in *The Serpent's*

Children or in *Mountain Light,* where it refers to a specific ethnic group. Here, the stranger is defined as he who is "in a strange land" (*Dragonwings,* 49); "the lonely man in a foreign land" (83). More consequential than the definition is the warning communicated to "the stranger" in the pages of *Classic of Changes,* "one of the Middle Kingdom's oldest books": "The three virtues of the Stranger are to be silent, to be cunning, but above all to be invisible" (23). In many respects, this admonition is disturbing. The stranger in the United States, the outsider, the person of color, has been silent and invisible for far too long. But considered in a larger context, this philosophy is voiced in *Dragonwings* as a piece of cultural history from which to move forward. In the very telling of this story, Yep is breaking the silence and reclaiming the voice of the Stranger, making the invisible gloriously visible.

3. The Other Outsiders

The Mark Twain Murders and
The Tom Sawyer Fires

Dragonwings is not the only book in which Yep explores the value of dreaming. Letty, a minor character in *The Tom Sawyer Fires*, has her dreams just as the major characters do. Her opinion is that "everyone should have at least one dream. Most folks don't know they have the wings to fly."[1] The protagonist, the Duke of Baywater, concurs, but adds that "folks just insist on walking instead of trying their wings" (*Sawyer*, 60). Dreams are especially critical for those who are outside of the mainstream of society, whether because of race, religion, economic class, or some other reason. Yep is interested in underdogs, those for whom dreams are the only resource.

The Duke of Baywater, who is 14 in *The Mark Twain Murders* and 15 in *The Tom Sawyer Fires*, is a boy with no stability whatsoever in his life. In fact, he lives on the streets—a Civil War–era portrait of the life of the homeless. He sleeps on boards underneath the wharves in San Francisco Bay Harbor. When his pal, Mark Twain, comments on the squalor and the odor in the area, the Duke answers matter-of-factly that "sometimes they dump the garbage into the bay. Or fish guts and stuff. . . . You get used to it" (*Sawyer*, 30). He confesses further that he sometimes has to use straw out of packing crates to keep warm, or grovel through the trash to find old clothes. But his life is his own choice.

I thought Mark had been studying my vest, but instead he pointed at the backs of my hands. "And where did you get those scars?"

I hid my hands quickly. "I catch rats and sell them to the gamblers so they can hold fights between the rats and their dogs." I shoved the hard-boiled egg into my mouth and began working my jaws up and down.

Mark made a face. "It sounds like a terrible way to make a living."

"I'm my own boss, Mark." I eyed him. "I go where I want when I want. Can you say the same?" (*Sawyer*, 31)

Part of what is impressive about both novels is that the Duke is not singled out as a victim of hard luck. Instead, he is portrayed as a member of an entire sector of society that shares the same living conditions. The Duke was taught "the ropes of living down here" (*Sawyer*, 32) by a 14-year-old friend, who was later killed by professional thieves. Mark, like the homeless boys, carries guns. People gamble. Men get excited over the visit of a famous "exotic" dancer. There is the occasional hoppy, "or opium addict, who lived around the wharf whenever he was out of money" (117). The Duke reminds Mark Twain, in no uncertain terms, of the relationship between this world and Twain's work: "'And anyway,' I taunted Mark, 'where would you reporters be if most people weren't scum? No more robbers and murderers and no more people wanting to read about them'" (33).

During the period when the books are set, the summer and winter of 1864, Mark Twain was, in actuality, a reporter for a newspaper in San Francisco. Yep cautions his readers in the prologue to *The Mark Twain Murders* that "While the story itself is fiction, it is based upon actual events of that time."[2] Likewise, Tom Sawyer in *Fires* is a historical figure in his own right—a distinguished San Francisco fireman who claimed to be the inspiration for Mark Twain's fictional character.

As always, Laurence Yep's research is meticulous. One piece of research in particular is recorded both in his autobiography and in *The Tom Sawyer Fires*. Says the Duke to Mark Twain: "I wish you hadn't lost your newspaper job." Twain answers, "I quit on a matter of principle. They wouldn't publish a story I'd done about

a Chinese man getting beaten up while a policeman watched. . . .
And that's the pure, unadulterated truth" (*Sawyer*, 25). Yep tells
the reader of his autobiography that the policeman was, in fact,
an Irishman, as was the attacker (*Lost Garden*, 6). This detail is
important if only because, subtly, it reminds readers that the history of America is replete with ethnic groups who maintain
strong cultural identities—that "white American" is not always
as clear a label as it may seem. Yep understands that the ethnicity of the policeman and the attacker is meaningful even if it was
not stated because various groups, though "white," have different histories in this country.

Certainly Yep could not write about the Civil War period,
though his stories are set in San Francisco, without addressing
the issue of slavery. After a long-winded analysis in praise of the
institution by a minor character, Twain directs the conversation
to the heart of the matter: "That's a pretty enough speech, . . .
but slaves are human beings, not machines" (*Murders*, 82).

In addition to weaving much of his research seamlessly into the
stories, Yep sometimes includes historical footnotes for curious
readers. In *Fires* he mentions that even before the advent of the
telephone (and telephone books), San Francisco published
addresses in a city directory, which was one way that people had
of locating each other (56). Not surprisingly, Yep includes details
about San Francisco history: "Fern Hill later became known as
Nob Hill, when cable cars made its slopes accessible to the rich
who were nicknamed 'nobs'" (*Murders*, 13). When an antagonist
warns that the bottle he is holding contains Greek fire, Yep's
note explains that this "was a name given to different liquids created to cause fires which would be difficult to put out with water.
The idea is first credited to the Byzantine Greeks who used it as
a secret weapon in A.D. 673" (*Murders*, 138). And of special interest to coin collectors, Yep notes that "silver half dimes were coins
worth five cents. Nickels had not yet been coined in 1864"
(*Murders*, 29).

Interestingly enough, it was a coin that was, in part, the inspiration for both of the books. In *The Lost Garden*, Yep reminisces
about how years ago, while still working in his father's grocery

store, they found themselves with an old penny, which the
younger Yep kept as a curiosity. While conducting research on
San Francisco much, much later, "Things began to click. I
brought out the penny again and put it on my desk and eventually
wrote the books that became *The Mark Twain Murders* and *The
Tom Sawyer Fires*" (*Lost Garden*, 23). In the book, this one coin
leads to a bigger story about a Confederate plot to steal gold from
the mint—a plan that is historically documented but was never
carried out (23). Surrounding this plot is a constellation of events
including murder, conspiracy, and general intrigue, which all continues in the second book. The main difference is that fires caused
by arson, rather than murders, are at the center of the story.

Critic Delphine Kolker summarizes *The Tom Sawyer Fires* in
the following passages, which are quoted at length because she so
marvelously captures and conveys the nature of the characterizations and the feeling of both books. Speaking initially about the
Duke of Baywater (who believes that he is of royal blood and will
be found one day by his true family), she writes:

> He is street wise, and his name gives him a moral sense below
> which he will not stoop; hence, the respect his companions have
> for him. Tom Sawyer is a fireman. . . . Mark Twain is an out-of-
> a-job journalist, living hand to mouth, on the prowl for a good
> story. . . .
> The story is fast-paced, with near misses, intrigue, and dia-
> bolical cunning confronting the heroes. There are many
> humorous scenes, especially the one in which rival fire compa-
> nies rush to the scene to up their ratings, somewhat in the
> manner of the Keystone Cops. But it is serious business too, as
> the three extricate themselves from impossible situations in
> the nick of time. . . .
> There is added charm in the description of frontier San
> Francisco, where the populace is affected by the Civil War . . .
> and is attempting to construct a respectable town; in the histor-
> ical allusions and descriptions, the reader will be able to savor a
> bit of Americana.[3]

In complete contrast is a review such as Zena Sutherland's, in
which she contends that "It is also not quite credible that the

furious pace of the story is kept up for its three-day span. This has a modicum of historical interest, but it's far from the well-structured and smoothly written book that Yep's readers have come to expect."[4]

Sutherland's review is far from the overwhelmingly positive reviews written by other critics. Nevertheless, differences in opinion are instructive. They remind us that all readers simply do not share the same taste. The pace of these books is completely credible and enjoyable to those who appreciate this type of adventure. Sutherland's critique reminds us, too, that every one of any author's books is not a masterpiece. Furthermore, each piece is different, and it is not always fair to measure each against the other. Finally, every reader does not read the same story. Where Sutherland reads *The Tom Sawyer Fires* as a suspense story that is "overdone, stretched both in plot and characterization" (Sutherland, 76), but others might perceive the thread that connects so many of Yep's novels—the story of the outsider, as embodied in the following passage:

> "We're two sad specimens, all right." I nodded to Mark.
> This time when Mark reached out, I let him pat my shoulder clumsily. Without having to say it, I think we both knew we were loners: restless people who would never feel comfortable in a crowd—nor have a crowd feel very comfortable with us. "We'll make out somehow, you and me." (*Murders*, 55)

With all the adventure, suspense, and mayhem, these stories are still stories about people who must find strategies of survival, whatever they might be.

Kind Hearts and Gentle Monsters
and *Liar, Liar*

Like so many other Yep books, historical and contemporary, *Kind Hearts and Gentle Monsters* is set in San Francisco, this time contemporary San Francisco. Charlie Sabini, the narrator, tells readers that he and his friend Chris got caught up in the long ride from her house into the old Italian area called North Beach. After transferring once, we got onto the 30 Stockton. For an electrical trolley it made an awful lot of noise, whining and grinding its way through the stop-and-go traffic around Stockton, around the double-parked cars and vans, puttering by the combination post office and Chinese temple, and then past the fish markets with all the crabs and fish laid out on trays and all the delis with the ducks roasted a golden brown and the chunks of red cooked pork.

The bus skirted Washington Square, where you can find one of those incredible San Francisco mixes, a Chinese father and son playing with a water-propelled rocket, some old Italians on one bench, blacks on another. And just a lot of people sitting, eyes closed, with their faces turned toward the sun like fleshy flowers.[5]

This is a wonderful example of the detail with which Yep describes neighborhoods. In his autobiography he mentions that at one time, his readers could use his books set in Chinatown as tourist guides, they are so accurate and colorful. Such descriptions give a sense of the movement of a city, the sounds of the city, and the faces of the people who inhabit the city. But Charlie and Chris are not a part of the neighborhoods invoked in this passage. They even talk about not wanting to feel "touristy," opting to go to a coffeehouse frequented by locals.

The genesis of *Kind Hearts*, however, is not specific to San Francisco at all. The original title was *Yes Virginia, There Is a Godzilla*. It was changed because Yep and his publishers could not get the Japanese film studios to grant them permission to use the word "Godzilla" (*Lost Garden*, 107). The book grew out of an experience of Yep's in which he burst a child's illusion about the actual existence of the monster. Duane, the "monster freak" in Yep's book, likes Godzilla because "you can put him anywhere and he'll always survive—even win and make new friends" (*Kind Hearts*, 87). But most of the action in *Kind Hearts* does not occur just anywhere. It occurs in "middle America" as manifested in California. Chinese Americans are not the only "outsiders" about whom Laurence Yep writes. The other "aliens" in *Kind Hearts and Gentle Monsters* and *Liar, Liar* are white American teenagers who are marginal or misunderstood people in their own neighborhoods. They must sometimes struggle to survive, and friendships do not always come easily. And unlike the people at the end of the passage above, sitting with their eyes closed, Yep's major characters keep their eyes open steadily, using their teenage years to take in as much information as possible. One of the recurring themes is differences in "point of view"—the need to recognize that the world is full of people with various experiences and perspectives.

It is at the very beginning of *Kind Hearts* that Charlie begins this learning process, when he starts to realize that not everyone has had the positive experiences he has had in school. When he finds it difficult to believe that his friend Bernard has been teased and berated by classmates, Bernard informs him that there are reasons he has not been the target of this kind of behavior: Charlie fit in because he got good grades, lettered in track, held a student government office, and "got into all the right cliques" (*Kind Hearts*, 8).

Though Charlie had not realized that Bernard had been considered an outsider, he did realize that Chris was viewed that way and did not fit in at the grammar school they all used to attend: she talked back to the nuns; she did not hesitate to be the first to try smoking or wearing makeup; and she was not invited to any of the parties or dances marking eighth grade graduation (*Kind Hearts*, 5–6). By high school, both Chris and Bernard attend public school. Charlie, in contrast, attends Loyola, an all-boy's prep school. But, he explains that "it wasn't like one of those Eastern prep schools where a lot of the kids come from rich families. Most of the students at Loyola were the grandsons of ditchdiggers and scrubwomen and the sons of grocers and plumbers. For our families, Loyola meant the next upward rung on the ladder so a C was the equivalent of an F" (79–80). These are some of the basic myths of American society—pulling oneself up by the bootstraps, individualism versus relying on family connections, upward mobility, the value of education.

As the plot develops, it turns out that Bernard is more of a narrative device to bring Chris and Charlie together, forming a dual-gender protagonist team that should appeal to both male and female readers. (The same kinds of teams are protagonists in several of Yep's books, challenging the traditional dichotomy of girls' books and boys' books.) It is Chris, really, who challenges Charlie and helps him in his personal development by being blunt and direct in her observations about him. She asks him at one point: "Why is it that everything that doesn't fit into your nice, white, Catholic, middle-class mold is *always* sick or weird?" (*Kind Hearts*, 27). When Charlie is adamant that "normal is normal," her retort is that "it's society that decides what's normal," what is considered savage and considered civilized. By this point, Charlie is forced to admit that "Chris seemed to have a knack for unsettling me and making me feel uncertain about things I always took for granted" (27).

It is notable, however, that there are adults as well who play a role in educating Charlie and challenging his ideas. Charlie happens to have a history teacher who is just as open, or at least as healthily cynical, as Chris is. He does not stop at informing his students that the local library was built by Andrew Carnegie, but informs them as well that Carnegie "had robbed his own steelworkers blind and then felt so guilty that he had gone around the country building libraries like the Boyd Street Branch" (*Kind Hearts*, 52). Though Yep does not linger on this scene, it is enough to include such small but strategically placed intellectual challenges to his readers. These few words about Carnegie fit with the other issues he raises about American values and about how Charlie—whom Chris places in the category of "All-American boy wonders" (77)—fits into this society.

Chris cannot be concerned always with the higher ideals of society. Rather, she is concerned most often with how some of these attitudes are manifested in everyday life. This is, of course, one of Yep's concerns, too. Much of the book has to do with how adolescents just entering high school manage their still-forming identities. One week the characters are writing immature chain letters, and the next they are arranging double dates in an effort to ease into the world of romantic relationships. Undoubtedly, too, they are all dealing with their family relationships.

Chris's particular struggle is with her mother. As the story progresses, it is clear that a large part of her concern with the notion of normalcy stems from her perception that her mother, because of her mental imbalance, is a monster of a kind. During a time of life when self-concept is of special concern, Chris has a mother who is liable at any moment, and in front of anyone, to accuse her of behaving "like a little fool" (*Kind Hearts*, 41); ask her, "Can't you do anything right?" (43); or even question, "Do I have to do all your thinking for you?" (43). So as Charlie comes to know Chris better, his impressions of her from a distance—tough and funny—are placed into a larger context, and he realizes that she has "an ego that was only the size of a grape" (102). She explains why she plays jokes: "I just got good at distracting other people by making them notice someone else." She pantomimes shooting a pistol. "I figured it was smarter to make other people into targets before I became one myself" (102–3). She also shares her feelings about her dead father with Charlie. Remembering their shared afternoons at the zoo, she admits, "I used to feel so safe here when I was with my dad. It was like nothing could ever harm me" (75). The person who shielded her from her mother's often unpredictable and cruel behavior, her father was the only constant in her life.

Chris's memory of that relationship fuels a subplot in the novel revolving around her interaction with a young patron who frequents the library at which she volunteers. Shunned by his peers, his only friend is Godzilla, whose image, on posters and in doll form, fills his room. Through Chris's gift of a Godzilla magazine, Duane eventually finds a pen pal who shares his passion. Chris reasons that in Godzilla, Duane found a protector from the hatred and ostracism of immature classmates, just as she had found in her father (*Kind Hearts*, 88). Godzilla is a comforting, protective monster in contrast to Chris's mother, who is destructive and psychologically devastating for her daughter. Through helping Duane, Chris learns that she herself is not a monster either and that all monsters are not the same. She discovers that, sometimes, someone—including herself—who is considered a monster by others has a heart whether or not it is always visible.

Many of the characters in *Liar, Liar* have no heart, it seems, and again, are outsiders. Helping his neighbor, Marsh, out of a confrontation with some students from another school, Sean, the protagonist, contends, "Even if he hadn't been my next-door neighbor, I think I would have helped out anyway. I hate long odds—maybe because I'm such an underdog myself."[6] Sean considers himself an underdog because his family is dysfunctional. His parents are divorced and he lives with his father in one city, while his sister lives with their mother and her male friend in another state. As the story progresses the reader finds out that Sean has had at least one brush with the law following his participation in a burglary ring. Marsh is "the biggest joker in all of Santa Clara County" (*Liar*, 2). Beyond being a trickster, he is somewhat of a rebel without a cause, his constant refrain to Sean being variations of "You're smart enough to know there are strings even if you can't see them" (8) and "We've got to destroy all the labels and the strings" (10).

Unfortunately, Marsh does not live long enough to contribute to changing any of society's faults. He dies in an automobile accident that Sean suspects was engineered by Russ Towers in his anger over a prank played on him by Sean and Marsh. The body of the novel revolves around Sean's quest to prove Russ Towers's guilt. Towers is a mysterious character throughout the book. The reader does know that he is angry at the world after a negligent teenage driver caused the death of his own wife and child. Towers is indeed guilty of causing not just Marsh's death, but other serious accidents as well. This is the substantive information the reader has.

Sean's analysis of the whole matter has two facets. On the one hand, he feels that "it really was a disposable society in a lot of ways. Throw things away and don't worry about them. Cans, cars, bottles—you name it and we junked it. Even people like Marsh" (*Liar*, 41). Underlying these feelings, of course, is his sense that society has junked him as well, because of his past, which he seems unable to escape. When Russ digs up the details and tries to use them to manipulate Sean, Sean characterizes him as "someone who thought that everyone and everything came with a price tag and that he could afford to pay it no matter what the cost. And then I realized why: I was probably just a thief and a liar to him" (102). And later he says, "Yeah, I see: Slip up once and the world thinks you're a liar every time. But as long as you have money, you can get away with murder" (116). Russ, a wealthy and respected businessman, escapes the suspicions of "society."

Critic Carol Billman argued in the *New York Times Book Review* that *Liar, Liar* "is primarily a mystery and not a novel about shaky family relationships."[7] Bill Erbes argued that "the plot is contrived and difficult to accept" and that "overall [the book] is pretty flimsy."[8] And though Denise Wilms contends that "Yep's fast-paced suspense story is weakened by forcing the issue of Sean's credibility," she gives the book, overall, a more positive evaluation, concluding that "still, the suspense is taut, and the conclusion, in which Sean and Towers battle it out, is worth waiting for. Dialogue is crisp, and Sean is a sympathetic victim who matures over the course of the story. This is effective escapist fare that should prove popular with junior high school audiences."[9]

This last critique is probably more on target than the others for several reasons. First, with the rapidly changing and more and more violent and bizarre society in which we live, to many young readers almost no plot will seem contrived. And even if the book's focus is not on shaky family relationships, it is on the shaky state of the society and some of the overlooked individuals in society. The book addresses the notion of the "neat little fairy-tale world in the suburbs" (*Liar*, 44). Sean thinks with disgust, "Murders were what happened in San Francisco, not in a nice little town like Almaden" (44). He talks about "fringe kids" (52) who fit in nowhere. He, through Yep's consciousness, of course, invokes the image of the alien. Though most of his classmates feel no real grief at Marsh's death, Sean finally finds that he can share his pain with Marsh's sister: "It made me feel a whole lot better inside—like a Martian who finds out he isn't the only one stranded on this planet" (47).

At the same time, Sean and Marsh's sister, Nora, are guilty of stereotyping others. When they need to speak with a classmate,

Angela, about the whole situation, this conversation takes place:
"I tried to picture Angela in my head. But I could only remember
a kind of fluffy blonde. 'She's a sophomore, isn't she?' Nora made
a face. 'Yeah, she's one of these girls with teased hair and bubble
gum for brains. She's been carrying around the same romance
novel for months. I don't think she's gotten past page twenty'"
(*Liar*, 59). Clearly, Sean is still a young person working through
many ideas and issues. What matters is not whether the book's
plot is predictable but that it raises challenging questions and, in
the final estimation, is challenging and disturbing, with Sean
asserting that "when I finally got right down to it, I realized that
life hadn't changed all that much since people lived in caves. Go
against the tribe and you get tossed out of the cave away from the
light and the warmth and the laughter. And there you were,
alone with the stars and the moon and a darkness so cold that it
could chill you down to your very bones" (122).

Laurence Yep as Outsider and *Shadow Lord*

New York Times book reviewer Colby Rodowsky makes an observation that is applicable to both *Kind Hearts* and *Liar, Liar*,
though written specifically in reference to the former. He calls it
"a moving portrayal of two teen-agers reaching out to one another, changing and growing up." But it is another of his statements
that is most revealing: "Laurence Yep, who has written several
fine novels about Chinese-Americans, has with this book broad-
ened his scope successfully."[10] Part of the meaning of this statement is that Yep has shown that he is capable of writing about
white characters as protagonists as well as Chinese-American
characters. This is a statement that can be interpreted either
positively or negatively. It forces readers and other critics to confront the reality that not only does Yep write about outsiders but
that he experiences life as an outsider himself—as a Chinese
American in this society. But significantly, he is, from one perspective, an outsider, or alien, in the world of children's and
young adult books.

Historically, it is white writers who took or were granted license to write about those of other cultures—that is exactly what multiculturalism means to many in the publishing world. Instead of opening the industry to voices from various communities, multiculturalism has meant, and still means to some, having white Americans tell the stories of "others" instead of having "others" writing their own stories. This is an arrogant and ethnocentric stance. What is going on when the opposite happens, when Yep writes about European-American protagonists? Is he making the statement that as an artist he can choose any subject matter he wishes? Is he attempting to reach out to an audience? Is he simply telling the stories he thinks should be told, making no big political statement at all?

Related to these questions is Jeffery Paul Chan's forceful assertion that "minority writers work in a literary environment of which white writers have no knowledge or understanding. White writers can get away with writing for themselves. At some point minority writers are asked for whom they are writing, and in answering that question they must decide who they are."[11]

One of the places where Yep talks about who he is is in *Shadow Lord*, his contribution to the Star Trek series of novels. In talking about how his writing has been characterized, Yep says that "I've been called a lot of different things in my lifetime, including a new wave writer." He goes on to explain that in the 1990s, new wave refers to cyber-punk. "It's really dark, enclosed universes that I find very depressing. I mean, they're entropic. The energy's winding down, you don't trust the government, you don't trust anyone. It's everybody for themselves; it's very dark . . . a gritty kind of writing and outlook. I'm basically a Star Trek person."

Star Trek novels, in comparison to cyber-punk, are characterized by hopeful endings with harmony between cultures. Likewise, at its foundation, *Shadow Lord* is about shaping a new kind of world and new kinds of societies, technologically, culturally, and spiritually. Says Vikram, one of the protagonists, "This is a world where the majority of people still believe that our world is at the center of the universe and all our stars and planets revolve around it."[12] This view could be construed as a comment on the problem of ethnocentrism and by extension the publishing world and the problem of most stories being told from a Eurocentric perspective. Toward the opposite end of the spectrum from homogeneity is heterogeneity, which, too, can exist in an extreme state. Says Vikram of his ancestral home: "Angira is one world only in the loosest sense. The average person here really identifies with his own clan first and Angira second" (*Lord*, 50). The country named in this passage could just as well be the United States.

Mr. Spock and Lt. Sulu are both defined in *Shadow Lord* as marginal men (30), belonging fully to neither one culture nor another, a status that Yep himself has experienced, as revealed in his autobiography. Like Yep, Spock and Sulu exist "on the border between two cultures" (31). But to them and to Yep, this is the most exciting, promising place to stand: "As painful as life on the border may be, it is the place where change first begins for a culture; and something new and better can be created" (35). "The ultimate objective of knowledge is to learn about one's self; and one can learn the most where two cultural identities overlap and where they differ" (251). They believe that a modern world can be created "that will respect your cultural integrity" (224). And perhaps most to the point, in Spock's words: "Truth has many faces and the seeker must be flexible. . . . To insist on knowing just one face is not to know it at all" (251).

Most American writers "of color" know many of the faces of this society. They have no choice if they and their talents are to flourish. Laurence Yep knows the dominant culture through interaction and through literature as well. Mark Twain's legacy belongs to Yep just as Chinese folklore is his inheritance. Critics should not consider him limited in scope if he chooses to write only about Chinese Americans. And it is no particular achievement on Yep's part to write about white characters. His achievement is addressing the issues he chooses, using whatever characters make most sense in each instance. He can employ heterogenous characters because he knows them and their cultures; he is not simply imagining. Imagining may have wondrous results for fantasy and science fiction, but it does not work for realistic fiction. Yep's track record suggests that he can write provocatively, if not entirely successfully, in whatever genre he chooses.

Shadow Lord received reviews that varied widely in their appraisals. Reviewer W. D. Stevens argues that the book is "a disappointment." His major criticism is that "the story lunges from violent action to philosophical discourse and back again. While the heroes are fleeing a murderous mob at their heels and reminding each other that they have to escape, they manage to stop and exchange conversation for the better part of two chapters."[13] Roberta Rogow, in contrast, writes that "Yep's writing is always interesting, often moving, and never dull." She continues, "This is one novel that can be read by science fiction fans who are not necessarily Trekkers."[14] This is the case precisely because of the "philosophical discourse" that Stevens decries. Yep's adventure stories are not full of action alone but have something substantive to offer readers. As Mr. Spock contends: "It is always instructive to see how a borderer survives and meets challenges—and even triumphs over them" (*Lord*, 251). The characters of *The Mark Twain Murders*, *The Tom Sawyer Fires*, *Kind Hearts and Gentle Monsters*, and *Liar, Liar* are outsiders and aliens in their own way, though they are white Americans. Yep understands their experience.

4. Children of the Owl: The Idea of Identity

Child of the Owl

Laurence Yep writes about outsiders and aliens not only in his novels, but in his short stories and picture books as well. His award-winning science fiction story "The Selchey Kids," also his first published piece, is particularly striking and disturbing, too. The protagonist, Duke, does not start off as an alienated person, but as part of a family and a community until a devastating flood destroys his reality. "I kept away from the mob, walking to the opposite end of the hill which was now an island. I huddled on the spot, looking out toward where our house should be, under the water, wondering why I was the only one left in an ugly, confusing world and wishing I wasn't. Family, friends and even identity were lost in barely half an hour. I decided then that I wouldn't worry about friends or attachments or other natural things that could be so easily broken."[1] At this point, one of the few things he is sure of is that "I belong to the species of Man. . . . I have no identity, only the inheritance of my humanity" ("Selchey," 94).

As the story unfolds, however, Duke's very humanity is called into question when Uncle Noe (Dr. Noe Selchey, a scientist and friend of Duke's parents) decides to let Duke know who he is ("Selchey," 97). Or perhaps, *what* he is: the product of "Director Noe Selchey's spermatazoa [sic] and a dolphin ovum carefully developed by radiation" (103). But despite thoughts of suicide both before and after gaining this knowledge, Duke decides, "I had come two thousand miles to find myself in the city and on the City I would build something new" (107). This decision is largely based on the relationship that Duke forms with one of his half sisters, Pryn. Her response to the idea of suicide is that "death is waste, death is the end of change and change is the purpose of man. . . . [Suicide is] not natural" (95). At the end of the story, Duke's own stance about the crucial concept of change is similar: "Man lives in the context of nature. He plays by the rules of the game but unlike other creatures, he can manipulate the game by changing the rules. Each alternation requires man to adjust again to the new game and on and on, ad infinitum. I've forgiven Noe because I understand the lonely man who hid in science" (108).

Though "The Selchey Kids" takes place in the future, it is still related very much to Yep's historical fiction and contemporary realism. It is related to those books with Chinese/Chinese-American characters as well as to those with European-American characters. His characters live "in the context of nature," but his books call into question what nature actually is. What is the relationship between nature and human nature? How do humans cope with change, whether environmental or otherwise? What is the nature of loneliness and individualism in the context of humans as essentially social beings?

Child of the Owl, an American Library Association Notable Children's Book, responds, to some degree, to all of these questions. The issue of loneliness (and aloneness) is particularly tangible for the 12-year-old main character, Casey Young, whose mother is dead and who has spent her short life traveling from one town to another with her jobless, gambling father, Barney. The real action of the book begins when Barney ends up in the hospital, where Casey sneaks in to see him even though the rules forbid children from visiting. When a nurse sees Casey, she knows that she is related to Barney because "You are the only Chinese on this floor." Barney reacts with a joke: "Gosh, I hope it isn't catching."[2] This is just a small hint that "Chineseness" is an issue in the story and that differentness and aloneness are issues as well—but not in the way that one might guess. Casey does not end up in a situation that makes her feel alone because she is the only Chinese—like her father in the hospital. Rather, she finds herself in circumstances where she is surrounded by other Chinese but does not feel that she is a part of them.

Because her father cannot take care of her, Casey first goes to live with her mother's father, Uncle Phil ("the Pill"), and his family. But when that arrangement does not work out, he sends Casey to live with her maternal grandmother in Chinatown. Casey is struck by the look of the place, the architecture. "But it was the people there that got me. I don't think I'd ever seen so many Chinese in my life before this" (*Child*, 26). The passage continues, speaking to the notion of stereotypes: "Some were a rich, dark tan while others were as pale as Caucasians. Some were short with round faces and wide, full-lipped mouths and noses squashed flat, and others were tall with thin faces and high cheekbones that made their eyes look like the slits in a mask. Some were dressed in regular American style while others wore padded silk jackets. All of them crowding into one tiny little patch of San Francisco" (26).

This passage is just as informative to readers as to Casey because it helps them to place Phil the Pill's family into some kind of context. His family is upper-middle-class and has an ambiguous relationship to Chinese culture. The oldest daughter, a student at the University of California at Berkeley, is "the president of the Chinese girls' sorority" (*Child*, 15). But because of their grandmother's Chinese lifestyle and worldview, this same young woman considers her grandmother "as superstitious and impossible to live with as anybody can be" (23). But the source of Casey's friction with this family is not culture, but economic status, which she feels is their overriding concern in life. Upon entering their home her first thought is that "the only thing in Phil's house without an expensive price tag was me, and they started to see what they could do about upping *my* value as soon as I got in the door" (13). But upon arriving in Chinatown, Casey realizes that there are many ways to look Chinese. The importance of this realization cannot be overemphasized, for Casey or for readers who know Chinese and Chinese-American people only through one-dimensional stereotypes, both physical and cultural. Casey realizes, too, that Chinese people can dress in many different ways and, by extension, that there are various ways to be Chinese:

> Barney and me had never talked much about stuff like this. I knew more about race horses than I knew about myself—I mean myself as a Chinese. I looked at my hands again, thinking they couldn't be my hands, and then I closed my eyes and felt their outline, noticing the tiny fold of flesh at the corners. Maybe it was because I thought of myself as an American and all Americans were supposed to be white like on TV or in books or in movies, but now I felt like some mad scientist had switched bodies on me like in all those monster movies, so that I had woken up in the wrong one. (*Child*, 27)

Thus begins Casey's struggle with her identity, which is also a struggle with her relationship with various family members. It is Casey's grandmother, Paw-Paw, who most understands Casey's feelings and helps her to work toward an understanding of herself. When Casey is most out of place in Chinatown, Paw-Paw interprets her feelings without her having to articulate them:

> "Did you feel that you were all alone inside?" Paw-Paw asked.
> I looked at her in amazement. "How did you know?"
> "All of our family go through that. I did. Your mother did too. We're all children of the Owl Spirit, you see?" (*Child*, 57)

What follows is a chapter-long segment of the story of the Owl, told to Casey by her grandmother. Though critic Marjorie Lewis thinks that the characters in Yep's novel are "strong and interesting" and that the book is "exciting and well-plotted," she asserts, too, that the legend of the owl is "strangely graceless and confusing."[3] Though this evaluation is valid—the story requires more than one reading even from sophisticated readers—it does not invalidate the worth of the story itself.

The owl story is composed of many intricate details and turns of events. But it raises several significant issues. It takes place during a time of hardship for both animal life and human beings. There is drought and subsequently a shortage of food for all, pitting humans against animals. Eventually, one of the humans takes an owl in human form as his wife, against her will. But "it was because Jasmine had never been an ordinary owl that she was able to adapt to her new life upon the ground" (*Child*, 77). Though she raises a human family and is dutiful to them, she is always an owl in her soul. Casey takes away a very significant insight about herself from this story that her grandmother tells: "And if I pretended I was an owl, I suddenly had some way of talking about my feelings because I felt like someone who'd been trapped inside the wrong body and among the wrong people" (82). Clearly, she is still uncomfortable with having a Chinese face and with living in Chinatown.

Fortunately, the story offers some insights more complex than Casey's about the issue of identity. For example, the ways in which the owl/woman had never been an ordinary owl are important. Specifically, she had never been the owl of Chinese mythology as described by Paw-Paw, a creature who does not honor family ties, going so far sometimes as eating its parents when they have grown old and useless. Jasmine, in contrast, does not agree with her other siblings that their mother should be sacrificed in time of hardship. She demonstrates the same kind of regard for family when she inhabits a human body, feeling satisfaction in the opportunity to nurture her seven sons instead of pushing them out of the nest when they were able to fly and survive on their own, as owls do (*Child*, 78). So though Casey feels that her Chinese body is the wrong body, the story of Jasmine offers some hope that she can, in fact, learn to wear this face with ease and even relish. This is a process that has begun already when she hears the story; she feels guilty when she uses a knife and fork rather than chopsticks, and she is beginning to enjoy drinking tea as much as Coke and milk (81). Her grandmother's mother-wit—"Your eyebrows are beautifully curved, like silkworms. That means you'll be clever" (31)—does not always sound strange. In short, she is beginning, little by little, to fit into the rhythm of life in Chinatown.

Laurence Yep is careful, however, not to romanticize China- town, just as he does not romanticize China in his historical nov- els. *Child of the Owl* makes it clear that Chinatown is not a monolithic community. In particular, there is definite tension between those born in China and those who consider themselves Chinese Americans (or simply American, as Casey does). Schools, both American and Chinese, are major sites of contention. At the American school, Casey thinks of other Chinese Americans as "those *Chinese* girls" (*Child*, 40) when they make her an easy target of teasing, knowing that she cannot understand their whispering in Chinese.

Language is also at the root of Casey's problems in Chinese school, an experience based closely on the experience of the young Laurence Yep: "Each week, we had a new lesson in the reader that we were expected to memorize, recite aloud, and then write out. So each week, I memorized a new pattern of sounds like a song and a new pattern of pictures like a cartoon. I wound up doing more work than anyone else in the class but I achieved my purpose: I passed without learning Chinese" (*Lost Garden*, 53). And like Yep's teacher, Casey's teacher thinks, "You 'Merican-born. Lazy. Lazy. Lazy" (*Child*, 41). Like Yep, Casey thinks of Chinese as "a foreign language" (43). But unlike Yep, Casey has no purpose, positive or negative, and finally "just gave up trying" (43).

Fortunately, critics have not given up on the classroom as a site of promise. Marla Dinchak contends that "while young people will enjoy [Yep's] books just for their stories, Yep's novels are also well suited for classroom reading." She goes on to explain that "Yep's skillful use of figurative language, symbolism, and other literary techniques make these books useful for teaching literary skills to junior high school students."[4] Dinchak contends, too, that the surest test of the power of a book is whether or not young people will want to read it. And she is confident they will wish to peruse Yep's work. If this is so, then there is hope that those who read Casey's story will, through reading and discussion, begin to think about major issues confronting American society. Perhaps they will bring more understanding to issues related to ethnic diversity and multiculturalism—what it means to be an American. These are some of the concerns that Casey is dealing with. They are not the only issues, however. She is dealing with issues, too, that are related to her family dynamics as well as her being of Chinese ancestry; what becomes more and more apparent is that ethnicity cannot be separated completely from any other sphere of identity and life. Yep, like Casey, is dealing with family issues, but through his writing. Just as Casey is concerned with communicating with her grandmother (who does speak English), Yep is concerned with communicating with his grandmother (who does not speak English). She is, tangibly almost, at the heart of many of his books. He notes in his autobiography that Cassia is an ancestor of Casey Young (*Lost Garden*, 54). Perhaps most telling is this admission of sorts: "As much as I tried to deny my ethnic background, I was unable to escape completely from being Chinese because of my grandmother, Marie Lee" (47). His grandmother, he often reminds his readers, is the inspiration for the character of Cassia. In addition to his grandmother, Yep bases so many of his characters on family members that his family has wondered aloud, good-naturedly, who Phil the Pill is based on.

What is apparent is that Phil the Pill has not so much to do with Yep's own family as he has to do with making the story of Jasmine, the owl/woman, multidimensional, with implications for the relationships between family members over the course of generations. Critic Sharon Wigutoff makes the observation that though parent-child conflict is a major problem for young people, writers seem to avoid it as material. When they do include adult antagonists, she asserts, "they are either invisible, shallow, lacking understanding, or preoccupied with their own lives. . . . We rarely gain insight into their thoughts and motivations."[5] But she is very clear that Yep's writing is an exception to these general observations.

Wigutoff is thinking specifically about Barney, Casey's father. But Phil is important, too. Like the Chinese owls that Paw-Paw describes in her story, Phil has essentially eaten his own mother, or at least thrown her out of the family nest. When she has a hospital stay, Phil and his other siblings all refuse to take financial responsibility for her. The sense that the reader gets, however, is that were Jeanie, Casey's mother, alive, she would have been the daughter, like Jasmine, who would have taken care of her mother. Though Paw-Paw has a chosen family in her social club, her telling the owl story to Casey is an attempt on her part to reestablish a certain kind of family tie, with her granddaughter. In the course of this process—getting to know her grandmother and the consciousness represented by Chinatown—Casey comes to know her mother in a way that would not have been possible otherwise. Wigutoff's words are doubly true. Not only does Yep create full parental characters, but full grandparental figures and adult figures in general.

Casey's father, Barney, is a central figure whether he is part of the action or absent. He is always a presence, though usually a negative one. His defining personality trait is that he is a habitual gambler. His gambling activity dictates every move that he and his daughter make. For example, one reason they move around so much is that once he owes money to too many people in one town, he must simultaneously flee them and find new sources of income and loans. To him, taking regular employment is a means of last resort when it comes to generating income. And in the end, Barney sinks low enough to become a thief, stealing something precious from his own mother and jeopardizing his cherished relationship with Casey, whom he "raised . . . to be an American" (*Child*, 129).

His ideas about wanting her to feel and be American explain why she has to learn his life story, his history, initially from others. Barney's old friend Sheridan tries to describe to Casey the social climate in the United States following the Great Depression when Casey's parents were a young married couple, with new high school diplomas. Explaining why Jeanie could secure a job while Barney could not, he offers this analysis:

> Most American bosses are men who'll hire a pretty Chinese girl just like that. . . . But to hell with some uppity Chinese boy. Let him stay a houseboy. . . . He took it for maybe ten years, but it

was eating away at him inside. And then, oh, I guess about the time the war ended, he said, to hell with it. See, it was like there was this brick wall in front of us. Some guys like me knew we couldn't get past it so we never tried. And you got your other guys who just went on beating their heads against it for years and years, but it was like Barney gave up because he'd paid his dues and now somebody owed him something. (*Child*, 108)

Sheridan and Casey then discuss who it was that Barney thought owed him something—God? The powers that be? What Barney found out for himself, no matter whom he expected something from, is that this society felt as if it owed him nothing past his high school education—not even an opportunity to put that education to good use.

It makes sense, then, that Barney would have some bitterness. What does not quite make sense is that this bitterness or anger is not against society, but against himself. He never reaches the point where he can admit that institutionalized racism has had a substantial impact on his life. Instead, he takes all the responsibility upon himself, internalizing the label of "loser." He is never able to reach a balance between understanding the societal roadblocks and yet taking personal responsibility for those aspects of his life that he can. He wants to believe in the promise of America so that his daughter can do the same. His reasoning is that no matter how bad things were for him, they "were still a helluva lot better than what men like my dad had to go through. Beatings. Lynchings. You know." His philosophy is to "worry about what happens today and not what happened yesterday" (*Child*, 128).

Ironically, it is part of Barney's philosophy, another part, that first provides Casey with a positive way of approaching her life in Chinatown. When necessary, she makes herself remember that he "had a knack for making me see the good side of things" and tries to convince herself that "there had to be something good to being Chinese" (*Child*, 44). In the end, though, daughter surpasses father in wisdom and understanding. He contends that the owl story is merely a story, while Casey draws meaning from it. She comes to the understanding that, like Jasmine, she can have several identities embodied in her various selves; that her identity is complex and multifaceted; that her Chineseness does not cancel out her Americanness. To be whole, she must acknowledge and embrace both her ethnic heritage and her nationality. Discovering her Chinese name, Cheun Meih, which means Taste of Spring, signals a corresponding period of rebirth in her life (143). Barney and Paw-Paw's children, on the other hand, in her estimation are miserable because they cannot reconcile the American and the Chinese images of the owl.

There is so much in *The Child of Owl*—mystery, parent-child conflict, identity crises, nostalgia, a bit of art history, American social history, and more. But at least one critic finds the afterword to the book just as intriguing as the story itself. It is instructive to consider this rather extended statement by the novelist Maxine Hong Kingston. She makes these observations:

> Laurence Yep himself has at least two voices, and I was enchanted that he tells a story-within-a-story about the owl totem of the Young family. It disconcerted me, however, when he adds an afterword in which the "I" is no longer Casey Young as in the rest of the book but apparently the author. He tells us that he has not actually seen an owl charm nor heard the owl story but made them up himself. Now in that afterword I believe Laurence Yep to be anticipating those critics—both Caucasian and Chinese-American—who will question whether his work is "typical" of the rest of us Chinese-Americans. So to all those ethnocentric villagers, he in effect, says, "No, I'm not misrepresenting Chinese customs. This is fiction." Good art is always singular, always one-of-a-kind, and an artist certainly has the right to make things up to write fiction—but somehow we expect Chinese-American artists to represent all Chinese-Americans in a way we do not expect of Caucasian-American writers. I hope that when more of our works gets into print that this burden—"Speak for me! Speak for me!"—we lay on each of our writers who gets published will become lighter. Laurence Yep has written a lovely novel that needs no apologies.[6]

The significance of Kingston's words cannot be overstated. As a Chinese-American writer herself, she is in a perfect position to understand and to articulate the literary, social, and political context within which Laurence Yep writes. *Child of the Owl* was published in 1977. The most prolific Chinese-American writer of young adult books, Yep has forged a career that in itself constitutes a response to Kingston's concerns, whether or not he was aware of them, whether or not he agreed with them. His many books demonstrate, powerfully, that there are many Chinese Americans, many and different Chinese-American experiences. No one book bears the onus of representing all Chinese Americans. *Dragonwings* accomplishes this, within the bounds the early twentieth century. *Child of the Owl* and later books accomplish it in the context of late-twentieth-century American culture.

Sea Glass

Yep himself reminds us that regardless of the social context or notions of an artist's responsibility, he, as writer, is writing for himself as well as for a reading public. He says this in reference to *Sea Glass*: "*Sea Glass* is my most autobiographical novel, but I can't always write that close to home because it requires me to take a razor blade and cut through my defenses. I'm bleeding when I finish, and I have to take time off by writing fantasy or something only marginally related to my Chinese heritage such as *The Mark Twain Murders.*"[7] This statement helps to answer questions, fair or unfair, about Yep's books with non-Chinese-American protagonists. And his words are so candid that the reader cannot help experiencing *Sea Glass* all the more deeply for having these insights.

The reader, too, experiences *Sea Glass* deeply because of the way in which Yep uses autobiographical material. He does not simply rewrite *The Lost Garden*. He reminds readers in the preface to *The Star Fisher* that he alters family stories in such a way that they are blended together, creating a new, communal bio-fiction.[8] In his autobiography he talks about "soaking up things like a sponge so that years later" he was able to incorporate them into his books (*Lost Garden*, 49). These details are many and con-

tribute to making the texture of the books rich and the characterizations strong and appealing to readers.

The main character in *Sea Glass* is Craig Chin, who has just
moved to the town of Concepcion, away from his beloved San
Francisco. While Casey Young had to discover her Chinese heritage, Craig Chin is quite comfortable with his Chinese identity.
In Concepcion, there are "Italian kids. White kids. Black kids.
Kids like Bradley. But the only other Chinese boy down here . . .
was my cousin Stanley. . . . All the other boys were Americans
and bigger than us, though Bradley was the biggest."[9] The most
notable thing about this passage is that Craig uses the terms
Chinese and *American* as mutually exclusive. The term *Chinese
American* is not yet part of his vocabulary. Neither is it a part of
the vocabulary of the students at Craig's new junior high school,
who, as is clear to him when they nickname him Buddha Man,
view him as a foreigner (*Glass*, 44). After being scolded by Uncle
Lester, the owner of the store that Craig's parents are running,
for not speaking fluent Chinese, Craig concludes that "if the kids
thought of me as a foreigner, the old Chinese here thought of me
as an American" (44).

As interesting as Craig's self-perception is that of his cousins,
Sheila and Stanley, students at the same school. They want nothing to do with him, going so far as to make fun of him along with
the white students. He understands the "Western kids" (*Glass*,
41) behaving this way but reasons that because of their shared
Chinese heritage, Sheila and Stanley should not join in the
humor at his expense. Craig does not understand why Sheila and
Stanley never visit him in Concepcion's small Chinatown, if only
to buy Chinese vegetables. He does not understand why they will
not even consider going with him to visit Uncle Quail, a living
depository of Chinese history and knowledge. They cannot imagine learning to speak Chinese. Craig is right on target, more than
he is aware of, when he thinks to himself, "It was as if [Sheila]
had to go out of her way to prove to the others that she was different from me" (41).

An especially poignant scene unfolds when Craig asks Kenyon,
a white female friend, why she thinks his cousins would pretend

not to be Chinese. She gets right to the heart of the matter: "Because maybe they think the other kids would make fun of them. . . . Not everyone likes to be different. It's easier to be the same as other people. Safer too. Only you remind them that they're not as white as they'd like to be" (*Glass*, 201). Kenyon makes the sharp observation, too, that Craig seems "to like being Chinese." His answer is simply: "It's what I am" (200). But of course, the matter of identity is not quite so simple. Craig admits at another point, for instance, that though he assumes that he and his cousins should share *something* based on their common history, "I couldn't have told you much more about what it meant to be Chinese" (42). Reviewer Jack Forman is off target when he claims that "the first-person narrative is sensitive and perceptive—a bit too so for a character Craig's age."[10] His comment is representative of an all-too-common tendency on the part of adults, whether writers, critics, teachers, or parents, to be condescending and to underestimate the capacity of young people to be reflective and intelligent readers. Reviewer Mary M. Burns is more accurate in noting that the narrative voice is "totally engaging . . . carefully but not self-consciously wrought."[11] For even if Craig cannot articulate it, he does know, as Yep himself understands, and as Casey Young learns, that there is something intangible, yet very real, about that quality Yep sometimes refers to as "Chineseness."

What complicates Craig's experience even more than his cousins' antagonism is his father's hostility. On the face of it, the tension between him and his father has nothing to do with ethnic identity and has everything to do with a father wanting his son to emulate him in every way, in this case through excelling in sports. As critic Donald Kao asserts, "*Sea Glass* brings into question the whole concept of 'achievement and success.' Craig is not a star, yet he is a full human being who strives only for those things that make sense."[12]

His father's behavior does not make sense to him. The story is the same throughout most of the book—Mr. Chin drives his son to play basketball nearly every waking hour, though he is an abysmal player, and encourages him against his will to play with the boys at school as well. Even when Mr. Chin witnesses for himself the disaster it is, inevitably, when Craig plays basketball with his schoolmates, he sees only what he wants to see and deludes himself into thinking that Craig does have the potential to be a good player. It only puts more pressure on Craig to know that his mother won many medals in the Chinese Olympics that used to be held in Chinatown during her youth and that his father was nicknamed the Champ of Chinatown after becoming the first Chinese basketball player to make the All-City varsity team (*Glass*, 16). His wish for his son is that "with just a little work, we could make you an All-City player. . . . Maybe even an All-American" (26).

The word "American," it turns out, is all-important. For Craig's father, playing basketball is completely entangled with his notions of being an American. Playing the game well was his only means of gaining the respect of white boys. Acceptance followed respect. It was a point of pride to Craig's mother that though some *Western people* initially had no respect for the Chinese at all, "Your dad could play any *Westerners'* game and beat everyone" (*Glass*, 27). The question of whether or not the respect of the white peers was sincere or given grudgingly is not addressed; in a way, the respect of white people was not the only issue. What Craig discovers is that his father, like himself, had struggled with his own father over what, essentially, were questions of self, though couched in other terms.

Though many authors find it impossible to say which of their books are their favorites, Yep does not hesitate when identifying *Sea Glass* as his favorite: "It's about me and my father, and my uncle's in it, too." One aspect of the novel that reflects Yep's own family dynamics is the insecurity he felt because both of his parents were very good athletes while he was not at all athletic. In *Sea Glass* Craig finds out through Uncle Quail that sports are not and never were his father's first love. His first love, in fact, was plants. It had been his ambition "to know everything about plants" (*Glass*, 78). This was a goal that he shared with Uncle Quail as he sat drawing plant life. Uncle Quail was encouraging. His father—Craig's grandfather—was completely unsupportive, feeling pride in his son when he got attention from becoming an outstanding athlete. His reasoning, according to Craig's father, was that all the family's money had to be sent home to China. Thus, money spent on drawing was a luxury. Uncle Quail recounts sadly the result of this attitude: "And I watch what happen. Your father was a good boy. It was just like he close a door inside himself. No more books about plants. No more drawing. And . . . no more talk about knowing everything about plants. He even tell me he not care about that stuff. But I got eyes. I saw" (79).

This passage presages the capacity of Mr. Chin to change his attitude and behavior toward Craig. For no matter how different he and his son are in personality, it is clear that Mr. Chin knows how it feels to be pressured to give up something that one cares about. It is perfectly understandable to Craig, after learning this information, that his father's small garden is so important to him, though he claims that the garden is for the pleasure of his wife. This fictional garden, of course, *is* the garden in *The Lost Garden*—the garden of Laurence Yep's own father.

In this entire scenario, Uncle Quail's insight, his seeing, is unobstructed. It is useful to Craig. There are other instances, too, where his wisdom is instructive. For example, he is able to recount the history of Chinese people in California for Craig. When Craig tells him that he knows about the contribution that the Chinese made to building the railroads, he responds, "Hear me, boy. We Chinese did more, much more, for the demons. We built the levees that hold back the rivers in the spring, and we drained the marshes so the demons could farm lots of land. We worked their farms and their orchards and their factories. And you know how the demons repaid us?" (*Glass*, 137). What follows is more description and detail about interaction between European and Chinese Americans, consisting mostly of the struggle of the Chinese to earn a livelihood despite the ostracism and sometimes fatal violence of some white people. Uncle Quail remembers his father's conviction about the value of long memory, that if even one Chinese man "remembered what had happened, then we would have won a little" (139). Commenting on the value of longevity, his conversation with Craig continues:

"That's how I got my name. Because I keep my coats so long the tails get ragged. Like the quail. But quails, they may be poor and ragged, but they're one tough bird. They live on when all the pretty pheasants and nightingales have been killed. Somehow the quails go on living."

"And remembering?" I asked gently in American.

"Yes." Uncle lifted his head defiantly. (*Glass*, 140)

What Craig is thinking in actuality is that perhaps Uncle Quail is too tough and that his long memory is not balanced, not tempered by the reality that there are good westerners as well as bad demons. And initially, because of his memories, he is unwilling to allow Craig to bring Kenyon to his cove to go swimming simply because she is female and not Chinese either.

Kenyon is not completely innocent herself—she, too, is guilty of defining people by stereotypes. For example, when describing the clothes her mother likes for her to wear, she complains that they make her look "like I just escaped from a carnival." When Craig replies that he likes some of the things she wears, her thoughtless retort is "if you're a gypsy" (*Glass*, 91). Craig does not challenge this statement, but perhaps the thrust of the novel will compel some young readers to question Kenyon's comment for themselves.

Though both of them may be thinking in narrow terms, one of the differences between Kenyon and Uncle Quail is that Uncle Quail is an adult and Kenyon is still a young person. Craig learns from everyone in his life, but because of the closeness he shares with Uncle Quail, he somehow expects something special from him. At the least, he expects him to follow his own advice: "Of all the people I knew, Uncle had the best reasons for staying away from others after all the bad things that had happened; but it was also a funny thing that Uncle was also the last person who should be doing that. I mean, Uncle had talked to me about being open to the world. But it seemed that he preferred applying his words to animals and to things, and not to people" (*Glass*, 142). Craig *is* open to the world. He has internalized more of Uncle's teaching than Uncle is aware of. He has opened his eyes to the world of Uncle's cove, learning about the water environment—the separate pools and how they are connected by narrow channels of water—and he now extends this model to the rest of his world. He realizes that though he is Chinese, he is still in some ways connected to everyone and everything is this world by various channels.

In a related statement, worth quoting at length, critic Marla Dinchak offers an insightful analysis of Laurence Yep's use of symbolism. She suggests that one of the most effective features of Yep's writing is his use of metaphor and figurative language. She then notes the way in which symbols are used in each book, generally being explained to younger characters by older, wiser ones. Dinchak continues:

> As protagonists mature, they become more aware of the symbol and what it represents. Moon Shadow in *Dragonwings* sees the aeroplane his father builds as the symbol for the reach of humanity's imagination, the achievement of the impossible dream. In *Child of the Owl*, Casey comes to understand her own cultural heritage and dual identity through the little jade owl charm, symbol of her ancestor, the owl-woman. The ocean and a reef teeming with marine life become symbols to Craig which help him communicate with those he cares about in *Sea Glass*. As the young people become more aware of the symbols and their meanings, young readers also become more aware of symbolism and are introduced to an aspect of literature which may be new. Universal truths are presented to readers, and Yep tells them that it is not bad to be different, and they should be proud of who they are and where they come from. He shows readers the incredible scope of our imagination, and he shows that impossible dreams can come true. He reaffirms the importance of communication, and all of this is more understandable and believable because of the symbolism. (Dinchak, 81–82)

Sea Glass is full of symbols, including, in the end, sea glass—broken glass, the edges of which are made round and smooth by water over the course of time. Likewise, Craig's rough edges are being smoothed out by living his life. At various times he dislikes himself because of his weight or because he does not measure up to others' expectations. Before he realizes that he can be both Chinese and American, he feels as if he is not anything at all

(*Glass*, 46). When his father scolds him, he feels "all broken up inside, and all the little pieces were dissolving" (128). But by the end of the novel, Craig is comfortable with the many different parts of himself and understands that he is a special individual in the same way that no two pieces of sea glass are the same. What remains of sea glass, in Craig's estimation, is "the brightness and the clearness" (213). And in the end, Craig Chin, 12-year-old Chinese-American boy, is just as bright and clear as sea glass.

The Star Fisher

Laurence Yep is at his best as a writer when he is creating historical fiction. And though individual characters might be bright and clear, the same is rarely true of the historical eras that they inhabit, every period having its share of complex social forces. *The Star Fisher* combines interesting, engaging characters with the particular social circumstances of a Chinese family in small-town West Virginia in the spring of 1927. Published in 1991, it blends elements of many of his earlier books and his autobiography to make a new, successful story that was the winner of the Christopher Award. Winning this particular award is meaningful because nominated books are judged by both reading specialists and young people themselves. The award recognizes books that "have achieved artistic excellence, affirming the highest values of the human spirit."[13] Indeed, as asserted in the *Horn Book*'s review of *The Star Fisher*: "It is disturbing but never depressing, poignant but not melancholy, for the principal characters . . . are individuals with a strong sense of their own worth, facing difficulties with humor, determination, and pride."[14] And the difficulties are many.

Yep reminds his readers in his preface that his family's migration to West Virginia was not a unique experience, noting that "Chinese families refused to be confined to the Chinatowns on the two coasts and were searching for a place in America for themselves back in the 1920s and earlier" (*Fisher*, viii). He goes on to inform the reader that he has met Chinese Americans besides his own family who grew up in such states as Arkansas, Mississippi, and Oklahoma; *The Star Fisher* is their story as well.

Fifteen-year-old Joan Lee is the narrator of the story, which begins when she moves from Ohio to West Virginia with her parents and her younger brother and sister. When she arrives at her new school, the following conversation ensues with Miss Blake. Note that English is represented in italics, while Chinese is the standard.

> In a polite but brisk manner, she helped me fill out the form. *"Now, where in China were you born?"*
> "Actually," I said almost apologetically, *"I was born in Lima,"* and added, *"Ohio, not Peru."* (*Fisher*, 55)

Similar incidents occur over and over again because people assume, with no basis whatsoever, that she and her family are not American. (Yep might point out that this happens in the 1990s just as it did in the early part of the century.) Part of being American, as far as most white residents of the town of Clarksburg are concerned, is speaking English, and so this kind of interaction takes place:

> Mister Snuff lowered his hand slowly. *"She talks American."*
> *"Of course we do,"* Emily [Joan's sister] snapped. *"We were born here. We go to American schools."*
> Mister Snuff's jaw dropped open. *"They* both *talk."* (*Fisher*, 8)

Not only is this man ignorant of the grammatical rules of the English language, but in his ignorance has the audacity to berate Chinese Americans who do speak English. Moreover, Mr. Snuff is surprised that these Chinese American even speak—any language. His referring to them as "darn monkeys" (*Fisher*, 7) is not simple name-calling but expresses his conviction that they are not human at all.

Much name-calling goes on in this novel. Besides "monkey," the other epithet, which has retained its impact over time, is "chink." Again, the name-caller is Mr. Snuff, this time jeering, *"Hey, chinky-chinky"* (*Fisher*, 133). He refers to them, too, as heathens (137). Name-calling does not occur only in verbal form.

After the Lee family's new laundry is fully operational, a local merchant chooses to display in his store window a quite demeaning sign showing caricatures of Chinese people, pigtails and all, throwing irons at each other. In the middle of the sign is a new washing machine. The words underneath read: *"All the China- men want one. Buy one and you'll never want to go to a laundry"* (144). Joan and her family, however, are not the only targets of epithets and harassment. When Miss Lucy, their landlady and friend, defends them, she is characterized as a "chink lover" (138).

Miss Lucy, more than a bit reminiscent of Miss Whitlaw in *Dragonwings*, is the character who represents the "goodhearted white people." But looking further, Yep does a wonderful job of not placing characters or whole groups of characters into simple categories. For example, it is clear in the shop-window scene that those who are generally considered decent members of society are not so in all contexts. Yep relates this kind of question to the issue of socioeconomic class: middle-class status is not equivalent to decency. Respectability is a relative concept.

Bernice, a white, lower-class schoolmate of Joan's, values respectability. Ashamed of her own family background, Bernice expends a lot of energy and thought trying to be a part of middle-class society. As Joan puts it, "In terms of appearance, diction, and even their names, [Bernice and her sister] were more respectable than the respectable folks—as if that might change the town's mind" (*Fisher*, 93). But it does not change the minds of the townspeople to any appreciable degree, and it is significant that Yep demonstrates this in a scene set in a church. When a Christian woman at the big church social demands that Bernice get out because she does not "belong with respectable folk" (123), Yep's message is clear. Some of his more sophisticated readers might make connections between this scene and the scene in which Miss Lucy talks about playing her own small part, as a child, in the Civil War, wanting to contribute to ending "that pernicious trade" (76). Undoubtedly, this was a trade that was to a large degree justified in terms of religion. The common element between slavery and Yep's presentation of the church social scene is the theme of hypocrisy. Yep introduces the theme in a way that says, clearly, that no one segment of society is completely innocent of hypocrisy. No one is entirely "respectable."

Bernice is a very complicated character. On the one hand, she is very generous. For instance, her concern about befriending Joan is that Joan will be shunned by others when they see the two of them together (*Fisher*, 61). On the other hand, she wants to be a part of people who are capable of being this petty. However, this desire is quite natural for an adolescent; it is a theme that Laurence Yep returns to over and over again. Readers sympathize with Bernice, because Yep's characterization of her suggests that she will become more respectable as she learns to have respect for herself on her own terms.

Joan herself is working toward self-respect in an odd way. When she finds out that Bernice's family is made up of "theater people," she acknowledges that "theater people were . . . well . . . not very respectable either in China or America . . . and suddenly I could understand why the other poor girls shunned Bernice" (*Fisher*, 89). So the scenario involves not only middle-class people judging poor people, but all people, even within the same larger group making distinctions among themselves. This happens in every culture. Joan understands this. Furthermore, her tone comes close to suggesting that she accepts it; in her own culture, she would, in fact, have the social prerogative to look down on Bernice. At the same time, Joan is dealing also with her feelings about being (or not being) American. Thus, when she fears that her mother might embarrass her at the church social, she thinks of Bernice: "Even if she was theater people, she was still American. Would the disaster at the pie social make her think I was too foreign?" (116).

Joan learns several lessons from her relationship with Bernice. One of these is "not to let a lot of silly prejudices blindfold you. It was important to meet with the person and not the notion" (*Fisher*, 101). Another is that "it's funny how there are levels and levels of prejudice in the world. The red-faced man hated us for being Chinese; but he would hate someone like Bernice as well for being the child of theatrical folks—just as Mama would herself" (94).

At this point, Joan has the invaluable insight that these levels upon levels of prejudice are perpetuated endlessly in a vicious circle, which can be broken only with much work on the parts of the individuals who make up society. But ironically, Joan cannot be a part of this process until she has a clearer sense of who she is as an individual. While she defines Bernice as an American, her description of herself is not constant. She has reached the same point as Craig Chin, when he defines himself as Chinese American. Joan is still struggling. It is painful to her to admit to herself that she is incapable of telling Bernice about China because she knows as little about that country, that society, as Bernice does (*Fisher*, 64).

Joan, however, probably knows more than she thinks she does about Chinese culture, because like Laurence Yep himself, she has simply "soaked it up" in the course of being raised by Chinese parents; she is a child of the owl, like Casey Young, whether or not she realizes it fully. It registers somewhere in her mind when her mother explains how a given social transaction in Clarksburg might be handled in China (*Fisher*, 102). Though she is a bit skeptical, it makes an indelible impression when her father tells her that the washboard was a Chinese invention that was brought to America (36). Information such as this might be considered trivial to many, but a writer such as Yep understands that little details, like the fact that a given society was technologically oriented, makes a big difference to young people who are ashamed of or confused about their heritage. This small fact about the washboard will remain with Joan.

There are countless other details, facts, attitudes, and images that are Joan's inheritance from her parents. She will recall always the image of her mother, though not literate, busily working with the abacus to balance the family's financial records. She will remember always her father's "long, elegant fingers around her wrist—fingers that were better suited to painting and calligraphy than to being thrust into boiling-hot water" (*Fisher*, 10). The story within the novel, the story of the star fisher, is about a beautiful bird, temporarily transformed into a human woman, who is trapped into an earthly marriage that produces a daughter. The daughter, by blood therefore, belongs "to both the earth and sky" and "[sees] everything through a double pair of eyes" (72). Joan will take with her throughout her life an appreciation for how most people—herself, her mother, Bernice, readers—are all, in some way, star fishers: those who belong to two worlds, both of which are their birthright.

In his autobiography Laurence Yep characterizes himself as "a bunch of different pieces that had been dumped together in a box by sheer circumstance" (*Lost Garden*, 91). He is referring to the whole of his background: being a Chinese American growing up in an African-American neighborhood; being too Chinese for some white people; being too American for some Chinese; being the decidedly nonathletic child of athletes; being the descendant of Chinese people who in some measure considered West Virginia their home. He compares his experience to that of others: "Almost everyone I knew—whether white, yellow, or black—came from a single background. They were cut from one pattern of cloth" (91).

This is a surprising and in some ways disturbing comparison. For what the stories of the owl/woman and the star fisher are about is belonging to various worlds simultaneously while maintaining a stable sense of self. Writing so insightfully and sensitively about numerous characters who experience this kind of double identity, this dilemma of struggling both to belong and to be individuals, it is somewhat startling that Yep would not realize that those around him might be experiencing the same. The young people growing up around him are probably trying to figure out what it means to be African American or Italian American or Jewish American. Fortunately, Yep's characters question identity from many, diverse perspectives, and they discover that everyone has a story; that few people are cut from one pattern of cloth regardless of race, gender, religion, age, economic status, or ethnic heritage; that everyone feels in some way like a star fisher.

5. Conclusion

Laurence Yep is accomplished and prolific. In February 1994 he was awarded his second Newbery Honor for the young adult novel *Dragon's Gate* (the first one was for *Dragonwings*). In the year before, he released four picture books, enlarging his artistic range. For the creation of an illustrated picture book is, indeed, a different kind of project, in many respects, from the writing of a novel. Often, the pacing of an illustrated story is very quick; the characterizations are not always full but rely heavily on a specific trait; the author must take into consideration the interplay betweens words and images. Yep explains it this way: "You know, I had a hard time doing a picture book [be]cause I, I keep wanting to put in scenes and expand moments like I would in a novel, you know, but a picture book has to be stripped down." Further, as a writer of picture book texts, Yep has concerns about the illustrations that accompany his words. He points out to me the political maneuvering involved in finding the illustrators one might want because of the way that publishing house loyalties work. With some artists, even skilled ones, he sometimes worries that Chinese characters will be drawn with queues, which are stereotyped in his opinion, or with slanted eyes. But Yep is happy with the way that his publishers have approached the issue of illustration and how the art in the various books has come out. He has joined the ranks of picture book authors with mastery and grace.

Part of the gracefulness of Yep's craftsmanship stems from its roots in Chinese folklore, a major underpinning of all his work. In *The Shell Woman and the King*, for instance, he gives the reader some background information on the original tale that he is now retelling.[1] His major point is that the kings in the era of the Southern Han were known for being extravagant and cruel. The king in Yep's story lives up to this image. Because he desires the Shell Woman for himself, he captures her husband, threatens to torture and kill him, and demands that the Shell Woman perform three wonders in order to save him. In the end, the Shell Woman prevails, and the king is destroyed, by the forceful use of her intelligence.

The Boy Who Swallowed Snakes, created by Yep as opposed to being based on a Chinese tale, is also about the triumph of those with good qualities over those with evil qualities. And the book jacket commentary tells the reader that the artists, Jean and Mou-Sien Tseng, have echoed this theme on the title page.[2] The illustration there consists of poisonous animals—a scorpion, snake, toad, centipede, and lizard—surrounding the Chinese character symbolizing long life. This emblem was used in Chinese culture to dispel evil and disease. The story itself deals with an aristocrat whose fate becomes intertwined with that of a young boy after the boy finds that which the man is trying to rid himself of—a snake that is capable of amassing wealth but that is also potentially evil. When the snake does not prove harmful for Little Chou, and in fact multiplies in number, the man thinks, "If one snake could make me wealthy, how much could ten thousand snakes steal?" (*Boy*, n.p.). The moral of the story revolves around the narrator's observation that "the rich man's heart was greedy where Little Chou's heart had been pure" (*Boy*, n.p.). The snake, like an idea or money or effort, can be used to good or evil purposes. It is always imperative to consider context.

A part of putting anything in context involves having information and perspective. *The Ghost Fox*, Yep's most recent chapter book (for intermediate readers), explores exactly that problem. While Little Lee's father is away on his travels as a merchant, a ghost fox inhabits and attempts to conquer the soul of Little Lee's mother. While the fox, in the body of the mother, exhibits evil behavior in Little Lee's presence, he does not do so before the eyes of the extended family and community. Not being open to the full story or to perspectives other than their own, they question Little Lee's actions and attitudes instead of trying to understand him or believe in him. Thus, "He knew that everything depended on him. Up until now, the grown-ups had only made mistakes."[3]

Little Lee does find a way to rid his mother's body and soul of the Ghost Fox. And one of the neighbors who was most doubtful about him declares that she knew that he was a saint all along. But he pays no attention to her, focusing instead on what is important—enjoying a normal life again with his mother and his returning father. What Yep has focused on here, as in many of his books, is the capacity of young people to think, to feel, to solve problems, to create, and more. Just as the adults in *The Ghost Fox* fail to give Little Lee credit for his insight into and understanding of the events happening around them, such is often the case with writers of children's and young adult books and other real-life adults. Yep never makes that mistake. He believes in both the power of children's literature and the energy, potential, and intelligence of his readers.

The first of Laurence Yep's books designed especially for beginning readers is entitled *The Curse of the Squirrel*. The protagonists are Howie and Willie, two dogs who are brothers, and Shag, a giant vampire squirrel. Although appreciating Yep's imaginativeness, the reviews were mixed; Betsy Hearne, for example, said, "The fantasy has some wildly inventive elements, but they're tumbled together too fast and furiously; Yep doesn't seem entirely comfortable with the abbreviated style and structure of easy-to-read books. Still, this beats most classroom practice materials, with just enough spoofy humor and slapstick action to hold it together."[4]

Several of Yep's most recent books are picture books, too—*The Man Who Tricked a Ghost* (illustrated by Isadore Seltzer) and *The Butterfly Boy* (illustrated by Jeanne M. Lee). The former is a Chinese ghost story first recorded in the third century. The latter is based on the writings of Chuang Tzu, a fourth-century B.C. philosopher. It is this story that relates to the foregoing discussion. The butterfly boy, in essence, is not very different from the owl/woman or the star fisher; he is butterfly and boy, and both and neither: "There once was a boy who dreamed he was a butterfly, and, as a butterfly, he always dreamed he was a boy, and he was never sure which he liked better."[5] More important, this butterfly/boy is a reader; he observes, reads all that surrounds him, all that makes up the natural world:

> The world was like a book to him,
> and the fields and hills,
> the rivers and lakes,
> > were like pages full of words
> > —words that he understood as a butterfly
> but not as a boy.

> > > > > > (*Butterfly*, n.p.)

Unlike the butterfly/boy, Yep's readers can understand the words as young men and women. Yep's stories will help his more mature, sophisticated readers as they begin, too, to read human interaction. The butterfly/boy is in some ways totally ignorant of the rules and mores of society, and he does not seem to care. That is one kind of freedom. But another kind of freedom is to know the place of tradition, respect that tradition, and yet find a way to transform it and make it useful and meaningful in one's life. This is the accomplishment of so many of Laurence Yep's characters, across time and place. Finally, like the butterfly/boy, some of Yep's readers will read not just as people but as butterflies, reading and understanding from a place that is not tangible, that is spiritual yet real.

The Butterfly Boy serves as reminder that there is not always a clear or evident separation between children's or young adult literature and "adult" literature. *The Butterfly Boy* is in its own way as powerful and poetic as Yep's longer fiction. It is a gift to all readers and will, undoubtedly, cultivate an already established audience into a whole new audience for his writing: a young audience who will "graduate" to his earlier titles as they grow older.

This same universality is accomplished in his collections of Chinese folklore, whose audience cannot be defined by age.

Neither is his audience defined by socioeconomic class. If anything, Yep writes about and for "common" people. As he says
about his characters: "Because of the people I met in our store, I
came to have little patience with stories about rich and wealthy
people. Even before I began selling what I wrote, I was trying to
tell stories about characters who survive at a basic level; and now
when I look for folktales to tell, I usually look for stories about
ordinary people rather than about princes and princesses" (*Lost
Garden*, 31).

The stories in *The Rainbow People* are retellings of tales collected by Jon Lee in Oakland, California's, Chinatown during the
1930s as part of a Works Progress Administration project.[6] Yep
retells Lee's collected tales also in *Tongues of Jade*, along with
some gathered later in San Francisco's Chinatown by Wolfram
Eberhard.[7] Yep's introduction to each book and each unit is short
but useful, compelling readers to think about questions that most
of them have probably never considered, even in this age of multiculturalism. In the introduction to *The Rainbow People* he
stresses the point that there are layers and more layers to any
culture; that Chinese culture is not monolithic—some aspects of
Chinese culture can be viewed in a generalized way, but others
are specific to a certain region or subculture. He informs readers
that most American collections of Chinese folktales are taken
from many different regions and explains that "trying to understand Chinese-Americans from these tales is like trying to com-
prehend Mississippian ancestors by reading a collection of
Vermont folktales" (*Rainbow*, xi).

What matters, though, is that the stories be told. This is the
significance of the title of *Tongues of Jade*. It refers to the practice in ancient China of cutting pieces of jade—which was
believed to have the ability to preserve the body—to fit parts of
the bodies of the deceased. The tongue was one of the parts of the
body that was sometimes covered in jade, "perhaps in the hope
that [the deceased] would speak again" (*Jade*, vii). Yep thinks of
the Chinese-American experience as "a poem whose rhymes are
still unfinished" (*Jade*, 160), and that can be finished only by
writers such as himself, who speak for those who no longer can.

In 1976, under the auspices of the Council for Interracial Books for Children, a committee called the Asian American Children's Book Project was formed. Though approximately 5,000 children's books are published in the United States every year, the committee found only 66, published mostly between 1945 and 1975, in which one of the protagonists was Asian American. Critic Elaine Aoki would remind us that the committee's conclusion was that, with few exceptions, the books were "racist, sexist, elitist and the image of Asian Americans they present is grossly misleading." The predominant stereotypical image of the Asian American was that they are "foreigners who all look alike and choose to live together in quaint communities in the midst of larger cities and cling to outworn alien customs." In discussing developments in the world of children's literature in the era following the committee's report, Aoki soberly points out that "over the past fifteen years, Asian Pacific American authors have been largely nonexistent."[8] Laurence Yep is the one Chinese-American writer of books for young adults whom Aoki identifies as a producer of quality literature during the entire span encompassing the 1970s through the 1990s. Likewise, he is the only writer for young people mentioned in Elaine Kim's *Asian American Literature: An Introduction to the Writings and Their Social Context*.[9]

Yep himself points out that Kim's examination stops "before the recent explosion of titles for children."[10] This explosion, however, was mainly in the world of picture books, rather than young adult books, though this is slowly changing with titles such as Marie G. Lee's *Finding My Voice* (Boston: Houghton-Mifflin, 1992). Lee and Low Books is one example of a press owned by Asian Americans that is dedicated to publishing multicultural, contemporary American stories. Like Yep, they have concerns about the misguided efforts under the name of multiculturalism. Phil Lee offers an example of the problems that can occur in illustration: "The street signs that you see in the background of books set in China or Chinatown are often not written in Chinese at all. They're just scribbles—artwork that looks 'Chinese.'"[11] Tom Low adds: "We want to publish books that children of color can relate to, but also which all children will like. Ultimately, what we're doing wouldn't be multicultural if it weren't cross-cultural" (Sunyoung Lee, 35). In any case, Yep does not want to be "the only one." Moreover, he feels that it is imperative that not only the Chinese-American experience be recorded and told, but the larger Asian-American experience as well. Toward that end, one of his most recent efforts is *American Dragons: Twenty-Five Asian American Voices*, a collection of short stories edited by Yep. The writers whose pieces he includes are Chinese, Japanese, Indian, Filipino, Korean, Tibetan, Cambodian, and Vietnamese. Some of the writers are former students of Yep's. His current editor, Antonia Markiet, who has worked with him in some capacity since 1973, cites this fact as just one example of his enormous generosity as a mentor. It is her observation that part of his strength as an editor is that he does not allow his voice to intrude upon the voices of the contributors to the anthology. He respects the feelings and the integrity of the writers.[12]

William F. Wu, a Chinese American whose work appears in the *American Dragons* anthology (1993), is the author of an ALA Best Book for Young People, *Hong on the Range* (New York: Walker, 1988). Other recognizable names are Darrell Lum, Toshio Mori, and Maxine Hong Kingston. Their writings, regardless of the author's ethnicity, are arranged into groupings labeled Identity, In the Shadow of Giants, The Wise Child, World War Two, Love, and Guides. They address numerous topics that echo many of the concerns in Yep's own work. These include explorations of ideals of beauty, children serving as translators for their parents here in America, assimilation, historical information, the myth of the model minority, persecution in American society, interracial relationships, respect for elders and tradition, stereotyping, and being of mixed blood. All of the stories deal with Asian-American experiences from the perspective of young people.

Significantly, in the afterword to *American Dragons*, Yep speaks not just of Chinese-American literature for young people or Asian-American literature but of African-American, Latino-American, and Native American literature—literature reflecting all people of color, and ultimately, "a common humanity"

(*American*, 236). He sees writing in the same way as the characters in *Dragon War* view what is called the world mirror: "It reflects the many worlds of which ours is only one possibility."[13] To Yep, literature is the world mirror through which all people, all writers can tell their stories and all readers can see theirs reflected; it is the mirror through which all readers have access to the realities, fantasies, and visions of others. It is entirely appropriate, then, that the Children's Literature Association recognized Yep's contribution to the field by awarding him the 1995 Phoenix Award for *Dragonwings*. The award is presented each year to an author for a title published 20 years earlier that has lasting value and resonance across time and across readerships. This is a description that applies to Yep's body of work as a whole.

Laurence Yep is interested in the possibilities of literature and the possibilities of people. In that vein, he prefaces *The Serpent's Children* with KU, the eighteenth trigram from the *Book of Changes*, an ancient Chinese text.[14] Its meaning is: "The superior person rouses other people and nourishes their hopes."[15] Laurence Yep's plays, science fiction, picture books, short stories, historical fictions, and contemporary realism for young adults all have the power to rouse people and nourish their hopes; Laurence Yep is a superior person and a superior writer.

Notes and References

Preface

1. *The Shell Woman and the King: A Chinese Folktale* (retelling), illus. by Yang Ming-Yi (New York: Dial, 1993), not paginated.

1. A Garden of Dragons and the Lost Garden: Introducing Laurence Yep

1. "A Garden of Dragons," *ALAN Review* 19 (spring 1992), 7; hereafter cited in text as "Garden."
2. *Dragon of the Lost Sea* (New York: Harper and Row, 1983), 13; hereafter cited in text as *Lost Sea*. Selections reprinted by permission of HarperCollins Publishers.
3. Denise M. Wilms, review of *Dragon of the Lost Sea*, *Booklist* 79 (1 October 1982), 250.
4. *The Lost Garden* (Englewood Cliffs, N.J.: Julian Messner, 1991), 105–6; hereafter cited in text as *Lost Garden*.
5. Margaret A. Chang, review of *Dragon War*, *School Library Journal* 38 (June 1992), 144.
6. Joel Taxel, review of *Dragon Steel*, *ALAN Review* 13 (fall 1985), 25.
7. Hanna B. Zeiger, review of *Dragon Steel*, *Horn Book* 61 (July–August 1985), 459–60.
8. *Dragon Steel* (New York: Harper and Row, 1985), 79; hereafter cited in text as *Steel*.
9. Unless otherwise noted, quotations from Laurence Yep throughout the book are from an unpublished interview by the author on 3 May 1993 in San Francisco, California.
10. "Truman Made Racist Remarks Throughout Life," *The State* (Columbia, S.C.), 25 October 1991.
11. Maxine Hong Kingston, "Middle Kingdom to America," *Book World—The Washington Post*, 1 May 1977.

12.   *Thief of Hearts*, the sequel to *Child of the Owl* will be published in 1995. Its main character is the child of a white father and a Chinese-American mother, the now grown-up protagonist of the first book. The major theme is her search for identity.

13.   Charlotte Zolotow, unpublished interview by the author on 13 May 1994.

14.   Margaret A. Chang, *School Library Journal* 39 (July 1993), 109.

2. Puzzle Pieces of History

1.   *Sweetwater*, illus. by Julia Noonan (New York: Harper and Row, 1973), 5; hereafter cited in text. Selections reprinted by permission of HarperCollins Publishers.

2.   "Laurence Yep," in *Authors and Artists for Young Adults*, vol. 5, ed. by Agnes Garrett and Helga P. McCue (Detroit: Gale Research, 1990), 247.

3.   Brian Stableford, *Vector 78* (November–December 1978), not paginated.

4.   *The Serpent's Children* (New York: Harper and Row, 1984), 21; hereafter cited in text as *Serpent's*. Selections reprinted by permission of HarperCollins Publishers.

5.   *Mountain Light* (New York: Harper and Row, 1985), 83; hereafter cited in text as *Mountain*.

6.   *Dragon's Gate* (New York: HarperCollins, 1993), 248; hereafter cited in text as *Gate*. Selections reprinted by permission of HarperCollins Publishers.

7.   *Dragonwings* (New York: Harper and Row, 1975), 1; hereafter cited in text; on cassette (New York: Random House School Division, 1977); on record, filmstrip, and cassette (by Miller-Brody, 1979). Selections reprinted by permission of HarperCollins Publishers.

8.   "Writing Dragonwings," *Reading Teacher* 30 (January 1977), 361 (reprinted in app. 2); hereafter cited in text as "Writing."

3. The Other Outsiders

1.   *The Tom Sawyer Fires* (New York: William Morrow, 1984), 60; hereafter cited in text as *Sawyer*.

2.   *The Mark Twain Murders* (New York: Four Winds, 1981), vii; hereafter cited in text as *Murders*.

3.   Sister Delphine Kolker, *Best Sellers* 44 (December 1984), 360.

4.   Zena Sutherland, review of *The Tom Sawyer Fires*, *Bulletin of the Center for Children's Books* 38 (December 1984), 76; hereafter cited in text.

5.   *Kind Hearts and Gentle Monsters* (New York: Harper and Row, 1982), 96; hereafter cited in text as *Kind Hearts*.

6. *Liar, Liar* (New York: Avon, 1983), 2; hereafter cited in text as *Liar*.

7. Carol Billman, *New York Times Book Review*, 6 November 1983.

8. Bill Erbes, *Voice of Youth Advocates* 7 (April 1984), 37.

9. Denise M. Wilms, *Booklist* 80 (15 September 1983), 175.

10. Colby Rodowsky, *New York Times Book Review*, 23 May 1982.

11. Jeffery Paul Chan, Frank Chin, Lawson Fusao Inada, and Shawn H. Wong, "An Introduction to Chinese-American and Japanese-American Literatures," in *Three American Literatures*, ed. by Houston A. Baker Jr. (New York: Modern Language Association, 1992), 215.

12. *Shadow Lord* (New York: Pocket Books, 1985), 34; hereafter cited in text as *Lord*.

13. W. D. Stevens, "A Shadow of a Novel," *Fantasy Review* 8 (April 1985), 30.

14. Roberta Rogow, *Voice of Youth Advocates* 8 (August 1985), 195.

4. Children of the Owl: The Idea of Identity

1. "The Selchey Kids," *Worlds of If* 18 (February 1968), 93; reprinted in *World's Best Science Fiction of 1969*, ed. by Donald A. Wolheim and Terry Carr (New York: Ace, 1969), not paginated; hereafter cited in text as "Selchey."

2. *Child of the Owl* (New York: Harper and Row, 1977; Dell, 1978), 8; hereafter cited in text as *Child*. Selections reprinted by permission of HarperCollins Publishers.

3. Marjorie Lewis, *School Library Journal* 23 (April 1977), 73.

4. Marla Dinchak, "Recommended: Laurence Yep," *English Journal* 7 (March 1982), 81–82; hereafter cited in text.

5. Sharon Wigutoff, "Junior Fiction: A Feminist Critique," *The Lion and the Unicorn* 5 (1981), 5.

6. Kingston, "Middle Kingdom to America" (see chap. 1, n. 11).

7. "Author's Commentary," in *Children's Literature Review*, vol. 17, ed. by Gerard J. Senick (Detroit: Gale Research, 1989), 202; reprinted from *Literature for Young Adults*, 2nd edition, ed. by Alleen Pace Nilsen and Kenneth L. Donelson (New York: Scott, Foresman, 1985).

8. *The Star Fisher* (New York: William Morrow, 1991; Puffin, 1992), viii; hereafter cited in text as *Fisher*.

9. *Sea Glass* (New York: Harper and Row, 1979), 2; hereafter cited in text as *Glass*.

10. Jack Forman, *School Library Journal* 26 (November 1979), 95.

11. Mary M. Burns, *Horn Book* 55 (October 1979), 542.

12. Donald Kao, *Interracial Books for Children Bulletin* 11 (1980), 16.

13. Dolores Blythe Jones, "Christopher Awards," in *Children's Literature Awards and Winners: A Directory of Prizes, Authors, and Illustrators* (Detroit: Neal-Schuman Publishers, 1983), 65.
14. Mary M. Burns, *Horn Book* 67 (May–June 1991), 334.

5. Conclusion

1. This book is Yep's retelling of a Chinese folktale.
2. *The Boy Who Swallowed Snakes*, illus. by Jean and Mou-Sien Tseng (New York: Scholastic, 1994), unpaginated; hereafter cited in text as *Boy*.
3. *The Ghost Fox*, illus. by Jean and Mou-Sien Tseng (New York: Scholastic, 1994), 49.
4. Betsy Hearne, *Bulletin for the Center for Children's Books* 41 (November 1987), 60.
5. *The Butterfly Boy*, illus. by Jeanne M. Lee (New York: Farrar, Straus and Giroux, 1993), unpaginated; hereafter cited in text as *Butterfly*.
6. *The Rainbow People*, illus. by David Weisner (New York: Harper and Row, 1989), xi; hereafter cited in text as *Rainbow*.
7. *Tongues of Jade*, illus. by David Weisner (New York: HarperCollins, 1991), ix; hereafter cited in text as *Jade*.
8. Elaine Aoki, "Turning the Page: Asian, Pacific American Children's Literature," in *Teaching Multicultural Literature in Grades K–8*, ed. by Violet Harris (Norwood, Mass.: Christopher-Gordon Publishers, Inc., 1992), 113.
9. Elaine Kim, *Asian American Literature: An Introduction to the Writings and Their Social Context*. Philadelphia: Temple University Press, 1982.
10. Laurence Yep, ed., *American Dragons: Twenty-Five Asian American Voices* (New York: HarperCollins, 1993), 235; hereafter cited in text as *American*.
11. Sunyoung Lee, "Books of Many Colors," *A. Magazine* 3:1 (1993), 34–35; hereafter cited in text by author.
12. Antonia Markiet, unpublished interview by the author on 11 May 1994.
13. *Dragon War* (New York: HarperCollins, 1992), 263.
14. For further study, see *The I Ching*, or *Book of Changes*, rendered into English by Cary F. Baynes from the Richard Wilhelm translation (Princeton: Princeton University Press, 1967).
15. *Serpent's*, unnumbered page (see chap. 2, n. 4).

Appendix I:
Awards and Honors Won
by Laurence Yep

Dragonwings (1975)

Newbery Honor Book for 1976 (American Library Association)
1995 Phoenix Award from the Children's Literature Association, award-
    ed for a book published 20 years earlier whose value is enduring
Carter G. Woodson Award (the National Council for the Social Studies)
International Reading Association Children's Book Award
Runner-up for the Jane Addams Peace Award
Runner-up for the *Boston Globe–Horn Book* Award
Focal Award from Los Angeles Public Library
Notable Children's Books of 1971–1975 (American Library Association)
Best of the Best Children's Books, 1966–1978 (*School Library Journal*)
Notable Children's Trade Books in Social Studies (National Council for
    the Social Studies/Children's Book Council)
Children's Choices (International Reading Association/Children's Book
    Council)

Child of the Owl (1977)

Jane Addams Peace Award
Boston Globe–Horn Book Fiction Award
Focal Award from Los Angeles Public Library
Notable Children's Book of 1977 (American Library Association)
Best Children's Books of 1977 (*School Library Journal*)

Sea Glass (1979)

Commonwealth Club

Dragon of the Lost Sea (1982)

Notable Children's Book of 1982 (American Library Association)
100 Favorite Paperbacks 1989 (International Reading Association/
Children's Book Council)

Rainbow People (1989)

Boston Globe–Horn Book Honor Award for Nonfiction
Notable Children's Books (American Library Association)
Children's Editors' Choices (American Library Association Booklist)
Fanfare Honor List (*Horn Book*)
Notable Children's Trade Books in Social Studies (National Council for
the Social Studies/Children's Book Council)

The Star Fisher (1991)

Christopher Award

Tongues of Jade (1991)

Notable Children's Trade Books in Social Studies (National Council for
the Social Studies/Children's Book Council)

Dragon's Gate (1993)

Newbery Honor Book (American Library Association)

Appendix II:
Articles by Laurence Yep

"Writing *Dragonwings*"

Once some anthropologists found a primitive tribe whose artists carved statues of powerful simplicity. When the scientists questioned the artists about their art, the artists would not say that they had sculpted the statues; rather they claimed that the statue already lived within each block of wood and told the artist how to free it.

Something similar happened to me when I tried to write my novel, *Dragonwings*. The story of the early Chinese-American aviator seemed to tell itself to me, but it was possible largely because I kept children in mind as the main reading audience.

But before I can begin to talk about the story of *Dragonwings*, I have to explain my general situation six years before when I first began my general research. Trying to research Chinese-American history—that is, the history of men and women of Chinese ancestry who had been influenced by their experience of America—can be difficult; perhaps I can make some of the problems clearer by presenting an analogy.

Let us suppose a far distant future in which America has become poor and outdated and its men and women forced to migrate to other countries to find work. Further, let's suppose that many of these emigrants leave Mississippi to work in Iran. A very few of them settle there and raise children, and their children raise children. And then one of their descendants decides to write about his ancestors. It is from this scanty material that he must construct a picture of life in Mississippi three generations ago.

These were the types of problems that I first encountered when I tried to understand the background that shaped me. It took some six years of research in the libraries of different cities to find the bits and pieces that could be fitted into Chinese-American history.

I don't have the time to go into any in-depth description of that history, but I should briefly explain some of the general historical background that went into the making of *Dragonwings*. Most of the Chinese who emigrated to America were from Southern China. As a group, the Southern Chinese are culturally and linguistically distinct from the Northern Chinese. Because of immense troubles at home, these Southern Chinese came to America since they could send large amounts of money to their families and clans back home. And for a variety of reasons, including prejudice and fear, it was mostly men who came over. For some eighty years, from the 1850s to the 1930s, it was largely a society of bachelors, for when the original men grew old, they sent for their sons, brothers, cousins, and nephews to take their place.

But a small number of men were able to meet certain special conditions under American law and brought their wives over to join them and start families in America. They created a family society within the shell of the older, larger bachelor society. And this family society, with its determination to sink its roots in America, survived psychologically by selectively forgetting the past history of the bachelor society and the often violent record of confrontations between Chinese and Americans. Ignoring acts of discrimination that happened in their own time, the Chinese-Americans still maintained a discreet distance between themselves and white Americans, choosing to imitate their white counterparts within the confines of Chinatown rather than trying to join the Americans outside.

The third generation, my generation, grew up in households in which little or no Chinese was spoken and Chinese myths and legends were looked upon largely as a source of embarrassment. But now let me try to explain what it's like to grow up within a group that has tried collectively to forget the past and ignore any differences between themselves and others. I found that I was truly like Ralph Ellison's Invisible Man—without form, without shape. It was as if all the features on my face had been erased and I was simply a blank mirror reflecting other people's hopes and fears.

If I wished to see features on my face, I had to put on different masks that I found scattered about in Hollywood prop rooms. I could be pompously wise like Charlie Chan, loveable like Peter, the houseboy in *Bachelor Father*. I might be stoic and inscrutable like Cain in *Kung Fu*. Or I might be the sadistically cruel and cunning Fu Man Chu. The best I could really hope for would be if I left Hollywood for literature—then I might become the loveable, dependable sidekick like Lee in Steinbeck's novel, *East of Eden*.

When I tried to replace these stereotypes, I ran into other difficulties, I've already described some of the problems I met trying to find out about my ancestors, but even when I did find material on them, I found that the Chinese-Americans had been a faceless crowd for most writers, providing statistical fodder for historians or abstractions for sociologists. I could give the Chinese population in each of California's counties for a fifty year period; but I could not have told you what any of those Chinese hoped for or feared. I could tell you about the acculturation process as exemplified by the Mississippi Chinese; but I could not have told you what their loneliness must have been like.

One of the few early Chinese-Americans in my notes to have a name was Fung Joe Guey who flew a biplane of his own construction in Oakland in 1909. The scene of his flight seemed so vivid to me that it was easy to put it on paper, but trying to explain how he got to that field with his biplane was difficult because I could only find two newspaper articles, the September 23, 1909 issues of the San Francisco *Call* and the San Francisco *Examiner*.

Since I wanted to respect his historical integrity, I used his flight as the basis for my novel, *Dragonwings*; and to make my own fictional aviator, Windrider, seem real, I had to recreate the bachelor society itself. However, to do that I discovered that a writer must not be like the anatomist who dictates a record of facts and figures after an autopsy; instead, a writer must be like a necromancer speaking to the shadows of the dead. But in trying to conjure up these spirits from the Chinese-American past, I had no book of spells to guide me. There were no magical formulae, no special chants, no words of power.

If I wanted to write about the Midwest, I would have the work of writers like Hamlin Garland and Sinclair Lewis to show me how to create that space and time. If I wanted to write about New England, I would have Hawthorne and Thoreau to guide me. In their writings, I could find guidelines not only for setting up a fictional world but also its population. I would have a wide range of physical settings and atmospheres to use in making my fictional world. I would know how the people of the world talked, how they dressed, and the kinds of worries they were likely to have. But I have no such guidelines for creating the Chinatown of seventy years ago, which is the time in which *Dragonwings* is set.

So in trying to recreate the world of the past, I was like a child myself who must have the most basic things explained to it. The kitchen god, for instance, was a common god found in many homes and easily recognizable to a Chinese adult of that time, but like a child I had to learn who he was and how I was to treat him. Or if there was a piece of meat on a plate, I had to be told it was duck and that it had been prepared and roasted in a special way.

I had grown up as a child in the 1950s so that my sense of reality was an American one. Now I had to grow up again, but this time in the 1900s, developing a Chinese sense of reality. Milk and cheese had to become exotic to me. An American chessboard would have to seem odd because it would have the river line missing from its middle. The turning point in writing *Dragonwings* came when the checkered tablecloth on a table suddenly seemed strange to me, as if it were too cold and abstract a design because I was used to designs that usually filled up space. So when I chose to describe things from the viewpoint of an eight year old Chinese boy, it was more than simply choosing a narrative device; it was close to the process of discovery I myself was experiencing in writing the story.

But at the same time that I was developing my Chinese sense of reality, I would also have to discover what relationships would be like within that bachelor society—that lonely group of men who spent most of their adult years apart from family and home. So again, it was natural to write about this experience with children as the audience. What were personal relationships like among men who would work for five to ten years or longer before they could visit their families back in China? To all intents and purposes, their families were lost to them. And since I had no guidelines for writing about these social relationships, I would have to project myself back into the past and see how I myself would react to others in that same situation.

And the relationship with which I would most easily empathize would be the most elemental relationship, the relationship between parent and child. And since most Chinese-Americans were men at this time, it would be easiest to describe the relationship between father and son—with the mother present only in the emotions and memories of the man and boy. It was within the strong emotional context of this evolving father-son relationship that the boy's relationships to others would unfold.

Then, too, it would be easier for me to describe the relationship between the boy and his father if I could use the most honest and direct terms. I couldn't be like D. H. Lawrence who described a parent-child relationship in "The Rocking-Horse Winner" by telling the story of a little boy who sat on a rocking horse all day until he rocked himself to death trying to win money for his mother. To be able to write about the relationship in the symbolic way requires a thorough grounding in the basic ways a culture expresses love and affection; but I was unsure of even that much for the early Chinese-Americans.

Speaking more practically, if I kept children in mind as the reading audience, I would keep myself from wandering off into conceptual tangents such as the existential alienation of Chinese-Americans. The important thing, after all, was to give emotional form to the people of that world and not to play intellectual games. The novel would succeed in more fully recreating that world of the past if I could show how Moon Shadow and his father, Windrider, loved and supported one another.

Perhaps I should note here that when I speak of selecting children as the audience for *Dragonwings*, much of that was intuitive, occurring at a preconscious rather than a conscious level. But I had another reason in writing *Dragonwings* for children. Because children are inexperienced and new to the world in general, their vocabulary and their ability to handle complex grammatical structures are both as limited as their ability to handle abstract concepts; yet this same inexperience is also a source of special strength for children's stories. To write for children, one must try to see things as they do; and trying to look at the world with the fresh, inexperienced eyes of a child enable the writer to approach the world with a sense of wonder. (I think I can say this without necessarily sentimentalizing childhood if I add that the sense of wonder produces as many terrors for a child as it does beauties.) Adopting the child's sense of wonder is the reason why—at least for me—the texts of so many picture books approach the lyricism that eludes so many modern poets today with their jaded, world-weary tastes.

I wanted to utilize this sense of wonder when I wrote *Dragonwings* since I wanted to base a large part of the father's motives upon Chinese dragon myths. I could have given the father more ordinary motives. I could have said he was compensating for feelings of inadequacy by proving he could do anything that white Americans could do. Or I could have left the novel simply as a story of "progress on the march": the usual story of a farsighted person among shortsighted people. But the invention with which I was dealing was not a mousetrap or a bottle opener. It was a flying machine, a machine that most people were convinced was impossible to build even several years after the Wright Brothers' original flight. When I wrote of the aeroplane, called Dragonwings, I was actually dealing with the reach of our imagination; for the dream of flight extends far back in time.

The dream of flight has dominated man's imagination from the earliest times. On the cave walls of Lascaux, Stone Age artists attempted to paint a magical man able to transform himself into a bird with the power of flight—a concept which is still widespread in cultures around the world. The Greek legend of Icarus and his wax wings is well known, but of equal antiquity is the story of the legendary ninth emperor of China, Shun, who not only made a successful flight but returned to earth using a parachute-like device (Eliade, 1972; Nicolson, 1960). Later stories claimed that Solomon presented Queen Sheba with the gift of a "vessel whence she could traverse the air." And in twelfth century English tales, King Lear's father, Bladud, supposedly flew with feathered wings, meeting his death. but it was not until 1903, many centuries later, that the dream of powered, controlled flight was made possible by the Wright Brothers. To paraphrase Bronowski (1969), their flight was more than a technological triumph; it was an imaginative triumph as well.

Similarly in *Dragonwings*, Windrider's former life as a dragon symbolizes this same imaginative power in all of us. And so Windrider and his son, Moon Shadow, are engaged not only in the process of discovering America and each other, but also in a pilgrimage, or even a quest for a special moment when they can reaffirm the power of the imagination; that power in each of us to grasp with the mind and heart what we cannot immediately grasp with the hand.

Moreover, children's stories retain a sense of wonder not only toward the world but toward the act of writing itself. Children's writers still enjoy the magic of summoning people and creatures from their imaginations and giving them existence with words or pencil lines or printed colors. They are still in touch with the magical power of words and pictures to capture the world in a way that many who write for adults are not. Adult writers often seem too self-conscious of their own technique. With all the splendid and terrible spirits of myth or of past history to choose from, they would rather conjure up the necromancers of the past in order to talk shop, mistaking an overwhelming self-absorption for a sophisticated complexity.

I am not trying to claim that adult Chinese-American stories are impossible to write; but given my general situation and certain types of story material, it was best to write *Dragonwings* for children. Growing up as I myself did without form or shape, I felt as ghostly as the spirits of the dead and so by giving them form, I was also giving form to myself. And it was only by feeling and seeing and hearing and interpreting things as a child that I could do so.

References

Bronowski, Jacob. "The Reach of Imagination." *Modern Essays*, 2nd ed., Russel Nye and Arra Garab, Eds., p. 216. Glenview, Ill.: Scott, Foresman, 1969.

Eliade, Mircea. *Shamanism*, Willard R. Trask, Trans., 1964. Princeton, N.J.: Princeton University, 1972.

LaBarre, Weston. *The Ghost Dance*. p. 177. Garden City, N.Y.: Doubleday & Co., 1970.

Nicolson, Marjorie Hope. *Voyages to the Moon*. p. 10. New York, N.Y.: Macmillan Paperbacks, 1960.

Reprinted with permission of the International Reading Association from *The Reading Teacher* 30:4 (January 1977): 359–63.

"A Garden of Dragons"

I once asked a friend how many hours of maintenance her English-style garden required. She simply laughed and said that I was no gardener if I had to ask that. I think, perhaps, that I understand now—except my garden has grown green-scaled dragons instead of green-petalled snapdragons. For the last twelve years I have had those beasts romping not only in the garden of my imagination but wearing out a manual Hermes, an electric Olivetti, an Osborne computer and now a Macintosh.

When I sold my first science-fiction story at 18, I had always intended to use Chinese mythology in science-fiction as well as fantasy. Almost five thousands [*sic*] years have created layer upon layer of myth and a history just as deep. I thought it would be easy to use what I wanted.

However, at the same time, I wanted to respect the culture that had produced that rich, mythical heritage. I didn't want to plunder odd bits willy-nilly the way less scrupulous writers had. For me, it was the difference between archaeology and grave-robbing.

To my surprise, I found it difficult to understand a set of myths where there was no ultimate evil. Instead, the creations of light balance the creations of darkness; and a legendary villain can wind up in Heaven as a bureaucrat.

More importantly, it was hard to reset my mental gyroscopes to enter that Chinese universe. In our western cosmos, the supernatural and the natural are opposing and even antagonistic forces. The fantastical is synonymous with illusion and has no existence in the real world.

However, in a Chinese universe, the supernatural and the natural are simply the different ends of the same spectrum. In fact, Chinese fantasy stories developed not from fiction but from early historical writing. In order to explain historical events, such as rebellions and changes in dynasties, writers recorded strange omens. At first, they were short, prose narratives—as bland as a police report. When it came time for later generations of writers to write down the strange occurrences of their time, they began to embellish their own accounts with imagery and dialogue. In subsequent centuries, writers began to make up stories that imitated the earlier factual narratives.

I enjoyed doing the research, delving as carefully as an archaeologist. By 1980, I had re-calibrated my intellectual instruments and was ready to make the leap. I thought the perfect vehicle was a folktale that I had found in which the Monkey King captures a river spirit who has flooded an entire city.

It seemed fairly straightforward, so I tried to put it down on paper as a picture book. However, I kept asking myself: who was this river spirit, whom I had renamed Civet, and why was she doing such terrible things? Trying to answer my question made the story swell from 8 pages into an outline for 800 pages. It became obvious to me that I would have to do it as a series beginning with a novel called The Green Darkness—which was the name of Civet's forest home.

The story became a conventional fantasy novel in which children from our world find themselves in an alternate world based on Chinese myth. The Monkey King pursues Civet to our reality and during the battle several normal children from our universe are drawn back to theirs. After a half-dozen drafts, I thought the story was almost ready to send in. However, towards the end of the novel, I introduced two new characters, a dragon and her pet boy. They were such lively characters that they stole whatever scene they were in; and I realized that I had to tear up almost everything and rebuild the story around that dragon called Shimmer and her pet boy.

In the process of rewriting the story, I asked myself what was the source of the water that Civet used to destroy the city, and the answer came to me easily. I had just finished reading Sir Aurel Stein's own account of a journey across a dazzling white, slaty desert that had been the former bed of a sea. During that trip, slabs of salt cut through men's boots and the ankles of the camels as they traveled among the ruins—details that went into the novel. It seemed natural to have Civet steal a sea. Furthermore, there might be a clan of dragons living in that sea. With that as a starting premise, the story metamorphosed into *Dragon of the Lost Sea*. Once they were homeless, the clan would become refugees until one day one of them encounters Civet once again. In that manner, Shimmer the Dragon acquired not only the title of princess but a history as well.

There is a point in writing when I feel as if I have reached the crest of the hill. The journey's end may still lie a long distance away, but it is now all downhill. As part of that momentum, it almost seems as if the characters have a life of their own and begin telling me what they would do. However, a creature with a pedigree as long as a royal dragon's thinks she knows her story better than the writer. I have never written about a character quite so independent, even demanding, as Shimmer. She was tired of always having the human view and insisted on having her turn—down to the tiny, puny snouts with which we humans are cursed.

By now, I had been rubbing shoulders with Shimmer for a while and had begun to sense her flaws as well as her comical quirks. When it came to write the sequel, *Dragon Steel*, I decided to expand on her dilemma. Though she was old by human years, she was relatively young as a dragon. Since Shimmer had been exiled at relatively young age, she had only a rudimentary—and highly romanticized—knowledge of governing.

It not only fit what I knew of her character but let me root my fantasy firmly in history—for the best fantasy is nurtured by the past. After having read about the rulers of several continents, I realized that a title did not magically imbue a person with wisdom. Quite the opposite in fact. Some of the worst rulers had been no more experienced than Shimmer. However, the history provided examples of men and women who had risen to the expectations of their people, and how Shimmer meets her challenge is the heart of the novel.

Since I had tried to take an unconventional view of dragons, I also wanted to do the same with their homes under the sea. What could a dragon garden or palace look like? As an undergraduate at U.C. Santa Cruz, I had taken marine biology and oceanography courses and had been enchanted by the real undersea world. It would be difficult to come up with anything more grotesque than a hag-fish or more charmingly comic than a sea hare. To make the undersea dragon kingdom seem strange and exotic to the reader, I only had to go as far as the real ocean.

By now I hope that I have shown that fantasy and reality are intertwined rather than forces antagonistic to one another. Just because fantasy places natural laws in abeyance, reason does not have to follow physics out the window.

Instead, the reverse is true. Obtaining a magical object should be as challenging to the mind as it is to the body. For instance, how would you protect a great treasure in a vault warded by magic as well as by armies? The answer lay in numbers: to multiply it many times over. That then raised the question of how to find that treasure in case of an emergency. To find the true treasure, one must use a solitary object that was so simple and ordinary-looking that a thief would overlook it. That puzzle becomes the climax of the second novel.

Up to this point, I had been writing the novels based upon an outline and a fairly elaborate chronology of events that I had written for myself while creating *Dragon of the Lost Sea*.

However, I knew that an outline was not the skeleton of a story. It was a scaffolding inside of which the true stories could be fashioned. Since events or characters had moved in a different direction from the outline, I would revise the outline instead of making them conform to the outline.

It became clear to me when I began the third novel of the series, *Dragon Cauldron*, that I would have to rewrite the outline because it was necessary to kill off at least one if not two of the characters. If Shimmer and her friends keep escaping from trouble unscathed, there was no jeopardy. Without jeopardy, there would be no drama and little emotional truth.

By now I knew Shimmer and her friends were capable of great sacrifices, but I found it difficult to write about it—though I tried for six years. Nothing worked until I shifted voices, letting the Monkey King take over the narration. As an immortal, the Monkey King is naturally cheerful even in the most dire of situations. Tough and yet funny, his consciousness provided the right platform from which I could observe a world in crisis.

I also needed to change the outline because I wanted to incorporate some new Chinese folklore I had found. I have to confess that it took me three years to learn how to use the U.C. Berkeley library system, but when I did, I found a treasure trove of Chinese folklore, including flying mountains that appeared when the sun rose at midnight and the unforgettable, creepy Boneless King, who was born from an egg dropped by a snow-white dog.

Finally, I thought I understood dragons better. In the first three books, I had tried to capture their quirkiness and strength, but I had not caught their beauty or their gallantry. It was something I had glimpsed the more I read about them in Chinese folklore; and it was something I tried especially to put into the final novel, *Dragon War*, in which Shimmer's wit as much as her courage brings victory to her and her clan.

After four books, I know that there is a certain point in creating a world where you stop being the owner and become an observer instead. It's rather like having the title deed to a garden. That scrap of paper is significant only to the lawyers; the garden's occupants, the flora and fauna, could not care less what I call myself; and I feel lucky when they show themselves to me. As Mr. Collins in Jane Austen's *Pride and Prejudice* would gush, "Such condescension!"

When they have deigned to appear, the dragons have taught me that there is more than one way to reach the truth and more than one way to portray it. There is more than one way to discover a heritage and more than one way to explore it. Fantasy may be the longer path, but its rewards are far more satisfying.

Reprinted from *ALAN Review* 19:3 (spring 1992): 6–8.

"The Green Cord"

There are two sources of history for anyone who writes historical fiction for children. The first source is the adult version of history with facts and dates and statistics; the second source is a child's version of history.

Had I only read the first type, I probably would never have written *Dragonwings*, *Serpent's Children*, or *Mountain Light* (all Harper). But I grew up with stories about China. However, it was not the China of the travelogues; it was not the China of vast, ancient monuments. It was the China my father knew before he came to America at the age of eight. So it was China as perceived by a child and colored by memory over the years.

My father has never seen the Great Wall or the Forbidden City. His China was small villages; each village had its own distinctive architecture, depending on which country its men had found employment in. After working in that country, the men would return to their villages in China, and there they would build a home that imitated the houses of the prosperous in the country they had left—though in some places, these transplanted houses might also have gun ports to defend against bandits.

But the difference between my father's China and the China of the travelogues is the difference between a child's version of history and an adult's. Adult history thunders on a grand scale like a movie in cinemascope; but for all its size, it is still flat, and its actors are like ants except for a few close-ups of the stars. But a child's history is like a hologram that can be held in the palm, quiet and small but three-dimensional. It treats its subjects with an immediateness that makes them seem to live and breathe.

Adult history is full of dry discussions of abstractions, such as runaway inflation. But that was just a concept to me until I heard about how my paternal grandmother in China would have to pack a small suitcase full of paper currency just to buy a box of matches. When one hears such anecdotes, the theoretical becomes all too real.

The drawback in using a child's history is that it is based on a child's egocentric perceptions, which are limited by the very nature of the observer. However, what these perceptions may lose in scope, they gain in concreteness and intimacy with which other people can identify. If this is true of a child's history, it is even truer of historical fiction written for children. While the facts of adult history are necessary for background material, they have as much to do with the creation of a novel as a backdrop has to do with the creation of a play.

Dragonwings could not discuss the rise of the labor movement in California, but it could show a child's view when a group of angry white workers, who blamed the Chinese labor for their troubles, riot in Chinatown. Nor was there room to discuss psychological traits of the obsessive-compulsive; but I could write about a man intent upon building an airplane.

I first began thinking of the difference between a child's version of history and an adult's when I finally made a pilgrimage to West Virginia.

In our family's own personal story West Virginia is as much a mythical homeland as China, for my mother was born in Ohio and then raised in West Virginia, where my paternal grandfather

started a Chinese laundry in Clarksburg. Subsequently, my
mother's family moved to the nearby town of Bridgeport, where
they spent most of their childhood. Since my mother, my uncle,
and my aunts had left West Virginia for California when they
were all children, West Virginia, too, was a homeland constructed
from children's histories.

West Virginia was always a semimythical place of green, wood-
ed hills that rolled on endlessly. It was a place of four seasons—a
strange thing for someone like myself, since my own homeland of
San Francisco has only two seasons, wet and dry. Bridgeport was
also a little town full of houses with big porches which were perfect for children to jump from—even if that was forbidden. In
fact, a good deal of what my mother and my aunts and uncle did
was forbidden to children. Their mischief was a year-round activity. Winter meant sneaking into the back hills where grownups
could not observe my mother doing unlady-like bellywhops on a
sled. Spring was trying to avoid drinking those awful spring ton-
ics. Summer was escaping the heat by wading in the "crick" in
your underwear while you looked for arrowheads.

Though I haven't been to China yet, I did decide to go to the
second of my mythical homelands, West Virginia. When I did my
research for the trip, it was strange to go from a child's history in
which everything is brighter, bigger, and lovelier to the history of
adults. The houses, the "crick," the cellar's vanish. Instead, I
found the bare facts buried in books like bones in the dirt: wed-
ding licenses, birth certificates, and wills full of dates and lifeless
statistics.

Above all, I was dealing with the process of acculturation—a
topic in which the new wave of Asian immigrants have generated
interest. So it is useful to see what happened some sixty years ago
to other Asia children. But acculturation is yet another abstrac-
tion spawned by adult history; and as I found when I taught creative writing in the Asian American Studies program at Berkeley,
abstractions are useful for theoretical discussions but not for
writing stories that other people will want to read.

Both my parents faced problems of acculturation. But my
father, who lived in a white neighborhood of San Francisco, was

always within walking and—sometimes of necessity—running distance of Chinatown. However, my mother and her family were the only Chinese in the area until another Chinese laundry opened up in competition.

Of course, my mother's family would not have been the first group of immigrants to face the burden of having two cultures. But most would have solved the problem by clinging only to their old ways and language and pretending that they were on a little island that was supposed to be part of China. Or, as so many other American families have done, they could have thrown off their ancestral heritage and severed their roots to the past—a simple enough thing for my mother and her brother and sisters since the white children of the town quickly came to accept the laundryman's children on an equal basis.

However, my mother's family solution was to juggle elements of both cultures. Though they stayed Chinese in some central core, they also developed a curiosity and open-mindedness about the larger white culture around them. My grandmother not only learned how to speak English but how to cook and bake American dishes. Though it may sound odd nowadays, back then my grandmother's specialty was apple pies. In fact, my grandmother once bragged to me that her pies always fetched the best price at church auctions—Methodist or Baptist. I think my grandmother's ecumenicism helped win acceptance in that small white community. Even in her later years, my grandmother displayed a remarkable adaptability. She listened equally to traditional Chinese music and to American rock-and-roll. In fact, she actually liked the Beatles before I did, and she once told me that the Everly Brothers' "Wake Up, Little Susie" was one of the funniest songs she had ever heard.

In general, my mother's family carried out their various adventures and misadventures with a good will and a sense of humor—whether it was facing up to bullies in playgrounds or to real bulls in snowy pastures. Whenever I want to picture what it means for a "face to shine," I have only to remember my mother and my surviving aunt when they describe West Virginia.

More than ever, I think their solution is particularly germane to modern times. It isn't only immigrant children who must face the problem of adapting. With modern mobility, the flood of information through various media, and the rapid pace of change, we must all perform a similar balancing act each day.

So I find it useful to keep in mind a visit that my aunt made to West Virginia back in 1951. Neither she nor my mother—with their children's memories—could remember the address of their house in Bridgeport. Yet once there in the town, my aunt was able to trace her way back to the house. Unfortunately, she had not written down the address, nor was she able to give me directions on how to find it. To find the house, or the spot where it had been, she had to be there physically again. Since her visit, an interstate freeway had been built in the area so that new housing developments and shopping malls had sprung up where had once been farms; and there was even an airport from which one could fly to New York.

Through the kindness of the historical society, I was able to find the laundry, which had been replaced by a bank. I seemed to have perplexed the congregation of the church across the street as I took photos of the parking lot. However, I was unable to find the house in Bridgeport, which was a disappointment because I had wanted to check on something. On my aunt's visit she had knocked at the door of their old house and introduced herself. The present occupants had then asked her about this tenacious weed that they could not get rid of. They had chopped it with hoes, dosed it with herbicide, and dug up its roots with spades. But the plant kept growing back as if it were determined to stay.

It turned out to be a Chinese vegetable that my grandparents had planted so long ago. It had transplanted well from China to America. One purpose of my trip to West Virginia was to see if our Chinese vegetable was still prospering—and perhaps exasperating a subsequent generation of American gardeners. Though I can't be sure, I like to think that it is.

It may be something as simple and yet as indestructible as a weed that links us to our past and binds us to our dreams. Seed, cast into strange soil, may thrive and grow—just like children and just like their history. In fact, a child's history is about growth itself, not only in terms of the body but also in terms of consciousness. Despite all of its limitations, a child's version of history is more useful for writing than adult history.

Far too often, adult history reads like an autopsy report. Writers spew out statistics like a coroner examining a corpse. Or they array the facts and dates like bones upon a table and consider their job done. But a person is not just a skeleton, and history is not just statistics. So writers of historical fiction must be like necromancers summoning up the spirits of the past. Their stories must be inspired in the original sense of the word, for these writers must breathe their own spirits into their tales before their books can come to life. For these acts of magic they have children's history.

A child's history, like magic, never quite goes away. It is there, only hidden, like the laughter of unseen children in a garden. Magic and children's history can be cemented over but never buried. Adults can put up steel and lay asphalt, but their buildings and streets can never outlast magic and memory. Memory pays no rent and is assessed no taxes, yet its value is infinite. It is like the sound of a "crick" heard on a dusty summer afternoon decades ago in West Virginia. It is all the sweeter for never being seen, only heard about.

Reprinted from *Horn Book* 65:3 (May–June 1989): 318–22. Reprinted by permission of the Horn Book, Inc.

"A Cord to the Past"

When I reached adolescence, my grandmother began to worry that I might fall in love with a non-Chinese girl. When I would visit her, she would try to get me to go to dances in Chinatown. After she began to admonish me, I made a point of *not* going to dances in Chinatown.

One action could make me feel as wise as an American owl at the same time it made me feel as disrespectful as a Chinese one.[1] The tension is fundamental to a Chinese American's identity. In general, America and China could not be two more disparate societies. America stresses rugged individualism, independence, and a sense of competition, while a truly Chinese society insists on cooperation, interdependence, and a sense of community.[2]

As a result, Chinese Americans are drawn simultaneously toward two opposites. Conflict is implicit to a Chinese American identity.

So, too, is a sense of alienation. On the one hand, skin color alone will keep Chinese Americans from being accepted completely as Americans. On the other hand, they are too Americanized to be accepted totally as Chinese.

Some Chinese Americans try to avoid conflict and alienation by insisting they are solely American. However, denial is never a satisfactory means of coping and—like any psychological repression—produces its own problems at some point. Chinese Americans who insist they are only Chinese exclude themselves from the mainstream and perpetuate the stereotype that Chinese Americans will never assimilate. Conversely, Chinese Americans who maintain that they are Americans and not Chinese cut themselves off from the vitality of their heritage.

As a writer and as an individual, I have been drawn to the stories of those Chinese Americans who have learned to live with a kind of grace on the borderland between two cultures. If Hemingway appreciated a grace under a pressure, I admire the grace of balancing.

What first drew me to the story of Fung Joe Guey, the Chinese American aviator, was the scope of his mind. Here was a Chinese American who had built and flown his own airplane just six years after the Wright brothers had flown at Kitty Hawk. In fact, I did not incorporate all of his real mechanical achievements in the novel, *Dragonwings*—which included his own telephone system. When his fictional counterpart, Windrider, dreams that he is a dragon, it was symbolic of Fung Joe Guey's own imagination:

that ability to grasp with the mind and heart what he could not grasp with the hand.

My grandmother could display a charming flexibility of mind when her grandchildren's dating habits were not involved. In the 1960s, there was one radio station that broadcast an hour of Chinese music and news each evening. My grandmother was afraid that if she ever changed the dial, she would not be able to find that station again, so she left her radio tuned to it all the time. However, during the daytime, the station broadcast rock and roll.

As a result, my grandmother stayed one musical step ahead of her grandson; she had liked the Beatles before I did—though she thought the Everly Brothers' "Wake Up Little Susie" was the funniest song she had ever heard.

As a lively, independent woman, my grandmother was the opposite of Pearl Buck's passive, long-suffering O-lan and the other stereotypes to be found in American fiction and film. She was such a vivid force in my life that I tried to capture her in a novel.

My first attempt was *The Emperor of China Only Has One Ear*. In it, a Chinatown grandmother had a pet tomcat named after an emperor of China. However, this was in a period when there was a spate of novels about ghetto children and pet cats. I realized that the last thing the world needed was another such story so I junked that version.

Trying to write authentically sometimes requires taking a razor blade to my soul. At the very least, I had to overcome my own upbringing: I had been raised with the conviction that there were certain stories that were not to be told to outsiders and must be kept within Chinatown. Then, too, I had no literary models for writing about myself as a Chinese American.

I went back to some of my experiences as an outsider coming into Chinatown from a Black neighborhood. For instance, I hated my Chinese schoolteacher, and I'm sure the feelings were reciprocal. I thought I would have my revenge upon her by putting her into *Child of the Owl*. (Instead, I began to see why she might think I was lazy and disrespectful.)

I also had some of my mother's experiences when she came from West Virginia to San Francisco's Chinatown. The other

Chinese children made fun not only of the way she spoke Chinese but of the way she spoke English. She also drew the disapproval of Chinese elders because she preferred soda to tea and saw nothing wrong about playing basketball with boys.

As a result, I decided to make *Child of the Owl* my mother's story as well as my grandmother's. Because the narrator was a girl, I tried to be careful in her problems. The central question, of course, was her identity as a Chinese American.

Living in two cultures requires an ability to juggle both cultures mentally. One can see a five-year-old Korean American girl dealing with the UPS man for her mother who only speaks Korean. In Asian American families in general, older siblings soon acquire a kind of maturity because they must deal with responsibilities beyond those of their peers. Not only must they act as interpreters and middlemen, but in families where both parents work they must get dinner ready and baby-sit their younger siblings.

Nor can they expect much praise. By tradition, Chinese parents will not commend children for fear of spoiling them and inflating their egos. Thus, Chinese American children can find themselves performing double the work load of an American child but without any of the expected rewards.

At the same time, Chinese American parents can seem callous and even cruel in contrast to their Western counterparts. In reality, they express their love in other ways that are often overlooked from a Western viewpoint—often in long hours of self-sacrifice and isolation.

For instance, my grandmother came to America as a teenage bride and moved into an area of West Virginia where there were no other Chinese women for miles. Instead of collapsing into self-pity, she learned English to deal with the laundry customers. Not only that, but she learned how to bake American style. She once boasted to me that her apple pies were the first to sell out at church socials.

At the same time, she expected her children to live up to her own exacting standards. As a result, the strictest Western parents in Clarksburg would seem lax in comparison to her.

Star Fisher was an attempt to describe this tension in Chinese American families. Joan Lee and her mother are a blend of relatives and friends. Caught between two cultures, Joan feels like the ultimate outsider. Once again, Chinese myth helped provide a lens to focus on the experience. This time it was the story of bird-women who fish for stars and whose abilities set them apart within any village.

The tension between Chinese myth and American reality is a tension that I think is a tension basic to the Chinese American soul. Like a coiled spring when sprung, it allows the imagination to soar.

When I tried to deal with the very start of the Chinese American experience, I again found the tension of myth and reality to propel me into the period. In *Serpent's Children*, a teenage girl, Cassia Young, is a fiery rebel determined to drive the foreign Manchus from the throne. She and her brother, Foxfire, are ostracized for their racial views. In fact, they are not even considered human. Rather, they are descendants on their mother's side of a serpent. Instead of being ashamed, they take a stubborn pride in the story of their origins. When the terrible conditions at home drive Foxfire to California, they discover they can have a revolution not with blood but with money. *Mountain Light* continues their adventures as a genocidal war spreads from China overseas to the gold fields of California.

Because of my interest in myth, I had searched a number of years for actual Chinese American myths and folktales. I had never been happy with the fact that most collections of Chinese folktales had been gathered in northern China because most Chinese Americans come from southern China. As a result, those collections reflected Chinese Americans as much as a collection of Vermont folktales reflects people from Mississippi.

I was delighted then when I came across a collection of folktales gathered and translated by Jon Lee in the 1930s as a WPA project. These folktales were strategies for living. They provided the recipes for health and wealth. More importantly, they told how to turn defeat into victory, sadness into peace.

When I tried to retell those stories, I tried to be like a Chinese ghost. In Chinese ghost stories, the spirits slip in and out of bodies as if they are Grand Central station. I tried to do something similar with a folktale—trying to slip into it to see if I could make it breathe and move. When the process worked, the characters came to life, becoming people I knew in Chinatown, and I put those stories into two collections, the first called *Rainbow People* and the second entitled *Tongues of Jade*.

As an example of how essential Chinese myth is to my writing, I only have to look at my railroad novel, which was begun over 20 years ago. The first draft was started in 1970 at the same time as *Dragonwings*—and includes a young man called Bright Star, who much later runs the laundry where Windrider and Moon Shadow work. Bright Star's work crew is headed by a wily survivor named Foxfire.

If anything, I had too much to write about. I could not write *Dragon's Gate* until I understood the myth about the magical gate that transforms carp into dragons. That novel is almost finished now.

By now, it is obvious how much I depend upon myth in my work. It is the razor that helps me find the authentic truth. It is the force that deepens the meaning of a story and gives it resonance. Myth provides what John Fowles calls an umbilical cord to the past. At the same time that we work within the present, we can draw strength and energy from the past.

Recently I adapted *Dragonwings* for the Berkeley Repertory Theatre. In the course of rehearsal, the actor who played Windrider asked why he hugged his son, Moon Shadow, when he first sees him. We spent some time debating the matter, because a traditional Chinese father would not display affection in public.

Finally we decided that Windrider must perform the same juggling act in his family life as he does in his identity and interests. In a sense, Windrider is every Chinese American who must create himself or herself. Moreover, the process is never complete. Definition and re-definition take place continually.

What is important is to maintain some connection to the past to provide not only continuity but vitality as well.

Notes

1.   The set of opposites is a long one, extending from dragons, to the act of writing and even of sawing (the teeth of a Chinese saw cut when it is pulled toward the worker rather than pushed away as in an American saw). Dennis Bloodworth, in his book, *The Chinese Mirror*, lists other ways that the two societies are mirror opposites.

2.   See Philip Slater's *The Pursuit of Loneliness* (Boston: Beacon Press, 1970).

Reprinted from *CMLEA Journal* 15:1 (fall 1991): 8–10.

Selected Bibliography

Primary Works

Novels

The Boy Who Swallowed Snakes. Illustrated by Jean and Mou-Sien Tseng. New York: Scholastic, 1994.

The Butterfly Boy. Illustrated by Jeanne M. Lee. New York: Farrar, Straus and Giroux, 1993.

Child of the Owl. New York: Harper and Row, 1977; Dell, 1978.

The Curse of the Squirrel. Illustrated by Dirk Zimmer. New York: Random House, 1987; Random House (cassette), 1989.

Dragon Cauldron. New York: Harper and Row, 1991.

Dragon of the Lost Sea. New York: Harper and Row, 1983.

Dragon's Gate. New York: HarperCollins, 1993.

Dragon Steel. New York: Harper and Row, 1985.

Dragon War. New York: HarperCollins, 1992.

Dragonwings. New York: Harper and Row, 1975; Random House School Division (audiocassette), 1977; Miller-Brody (record, cassette, filmstrip with cassette), 1979.

The Ghost Fox. Illustrated by Jean and Mou-Sien Tseng. New York: Scholastic, 1994.

The Junior Thunder Lord. Illustrated by Robert Van Nutt. Mahwah, N.J.: Bridgewater, 1994.

Kind Hearts and Gentle Monsters. New York: Harper and Row, 1982.

Liar, Liar. New York: Avon, 1983.

The Man Who Tricked a Ghost. Illustrated by Isadore Seltzer. Mahwah, N.J.: Bridgewater Books, 1993.

The Mark Twain Murders. New York: Four Winds, 1981.

Monster Makers, Inc. New York: Arbor, 1986.

Mountain Light. New York: Harper and Row, 1985.

The Rainbow People. Illustrated by David Weisner. New York: Harper and Row, 1989. (retellings of folktales collected by Jon Lee)

Seademons. New York: Harper and Row, 1977.
Sea Glass. New York: Harper and Row, 1979.
The Serpent's Children. New York: Harper and Row, 1984.
Shadow Lord. New York: Pocket Books, 1985.
The Shell Woman and the King: A Chinese Folktale. Illustrated by Yang Ming-Yi. New York: Dial, 1993. (retelling of a Chinese folktale)
The Star Fisher. New York: William Morrow, 1991; Puffin, 1992.
Sweetwater. Illustrated by Julia Noonan. New York: Harper and Row, 1973.
The Tom Sawyer Fires. New York: William Morrow, 1984.
Tongues of Jade. Illustrated by David Weisner. New York: HarperCollins, 1991. (retellings of folktales collected by Jon Lee, partially collected earlier by Wolfram Eberhard)
When Dragons Weep. New York: Scholastic, 1994.

Autobiography

The Lost Garden. Englewood Cliffs, N.J.: Julian Messner, 1991.

Short Stories

"The Eddystone Light." In *Demon Kind*, edited by Roger Elwood. New York: Avon, 1973.
"The Electric Neon Mermaid." In *Quark 2*, edited by Samuel R. Delany and Marilyn Hacker. New York: Paperback Library, 1971.
"In a Sky of Daemons." In *Protostars*, edited by David Gerrold and Stephen Goldin. New York: Ballantine, 1971.
"The Looking-Glass Sea." In *Strange Bedfellows: Sex and Science Fiction*, edited by Thomas N. Scortia, 165–77. New York: Random, 1972.
"The Selchey Kids." *Worlds of If* 18 (February 1968): 88–108. (Collected in *World's Best Science Fiction of 1969*, edited by Donald A. Wolheim and Terry Carr. New York: Ace, 1969.)

Plays

"Dragonwings." In *American Theatre Magazine* 9 (September 1992): 34+. Dramatists Play Service, 1993.
Fairy Bones. Unpublished, 1987; new version 1992.
"Pay the Chinaman." In *Between Worlds*, introduction by Misha Berson. New York: Theatre Communications Group, 1989.

Anthologies

American Dragons: Twenty-Five Asian American Voices, edited by Laurence Yep. New York: HarperCollins, 1993.

Articles

"Author's Commentary." *Children's Literature Review*, vol. 17. Edited by Gerard J. Senick. Detroit: Gale Research, 1989, 201–9. Reprinted from *Literature for Today's Young Adults*, 2nd edition. Edited by Alleen Pace Nilsen and Kenneth L. Donelson. New York: Scott, Foresman, 1985, 426–27.

"A Cord to the Past." *CMLEA Journal* 15:1 (fall 1991): 8–10. (reprinted in app. 2)

"The Ethnic Writer as Alien." *Interracial Books for Children Bulletin* 10:5 (1979).

"Fantasy and Reality." *Horn Book* 54 (April 1978): 137–43.

"A Garden of Dragons." *ALAN Review* 19:3 (spring 1992): 6–8. (reprinted in app. 2)

"The Green Cord." *Horn Book* 65:3 (May–June 1989): 318–22. (reprinted in app. 2)

"Laurence Yep." *Authors and Artists for Young Adults*, vol. 5. Edited by Agnes Garrett and Helga P. McCue. Detroit: Gale Research, 1990, 245–52.

"World Building." *Innocence and Experience: Essays and Conversation's on Children's Literature*. Edited by Barbara Harrison. New York: Lothrop, 1987, 182–84.

"Writing *Dragonwings*." *The Reading Teacher* 30:4 (January 1977): 359–63. (reprinted in app. 2)

Interviews

By Dianne Johnson-Feelings. 3 May 1993. Unpublished.

Forthcoming Publications

The City of Dragons. New York: Scholastic, 1995.

Hiroshima. New York: Scholastic, 1995.

Later, Gator. Westport, Conn.: Hyperion, 1995.

Thief of Hearts. New York: HarperCollins, 1995.

Tiger Woman. Illustrated by Robert Roth. Mahwah, N.J.: Bridgewater, 1995.

The Tree of Dreams: Ten Tales from the Garden of Night. Mahwah, N.J.: Bridgewater, 1995.

Secondary Sources

Articles, Books, and Parts of Books

Cai, Mingshui. "A Balanced View of Acculturation: Comments on Lawrence [sic] Yep's Three Novels." *Children's Literature in Education* 23 (1992): 107–18.

Dinchak, Marla. "Recommended: Laurence Yep." *English Journal* 71 (March 1982): 81–82.

Fei, Faye C. Revision of "Between Worlds: Contemporary Asian-American Plays." *The Drama Review* 37 (spring 1993): 173.

Gok, F. "'Child of the Owl' Is No Shirley Temple." *San Francisco Journal*, 20 July 1977.

Huck, Charlotte S. "Contemporary Realistic Fiction." In *Children's Literature in the Elementary School*, 3rd edition. New York: Holt, Rinehart and Winston, 1979, 388–463.

Khorana, Meena. "The Ethnic Family and Identity Formation in Adolescents." In *The Child and the Family: Selected Papers from the 1988 International Conference of the Children's Literature Association*, ed. by Susan R. Gannon. New York: Pace University, 1989.

Norton, Donna E. "Multiethnic Literature." In *Through the Eyes of a Child: An Introduction to Children's Literature*, 2nd edition. New York: Merrill, 1987, 500–561.

Schirmer, John. "Cognitive Development Assignment: Building Bridges Between Chinese-Americans and Elementary School Classrooms." ERIC ED353162, 1991.

"School Touring Production Study Guide for *Dragonwings*." Berkeley: Berkeley Repertory Theatre's Programs for Education.

Stanek, Lou Willet. "A Teacher's Resource Guide to Laurence Yep." New York: HarperCollins, 1991.

Wigutoff, Sharon. "Junior Fiction: A Feminist Critique." In *The Lion and the Unicorn* 5 (1981): 4–18.

Yung, J. "'Child of the Owl,' A Wild Tale of a Girl's Experience in Chinatown." *East-West* 6 July 1977.

Interviews

Markiet, Antonia, by Dianne Johnson-Feelings. Unpublished. 11 May 1994.

Zolotow, Charlotte, by Dianne Johnson-Feelings. Unpublished. 13 May 1994.

Dissertations

Li, Leiwei. *Monkeying Tradition: Reconstructing Contemporary Chinese-American Literary Culture*. Ph.D. diss., University of Texas, Austin. Ann Arbor, Mich.: University Microfilms, 1991.

Lin, Mao-Chu. *Identity and Chinese-American Experience: A Study of Chinatown American Literature Since World War II*. Ph.D. diss., University of Minnesota. Ann Arbor, Mich.: University Microfilms, 1988.

Selected Book Reviews

American Dragons
Booklist 89 (15 May 1993): 1684.
Bulletin of the Center for Children's Books 46 (July 1993): 362.
English Journal 82 (October 1993): 82.
Kirkus Reviews 61 (15 June 1993): 794.
Publishers Weekly 240 (14 June 1993): 72.
School Library Journal 39 (July 1993): 109.
Vasilakis, Nancy. *Horn Book* 69 (September 1993): 607.
Voice of Youth Advocates 16 (October 1993): 237.

The Butterfly Boy
Kirkus Reviews 61 (1 September 1993): 1154.
Publishers Weekly 240 (30 August 1993): 96.

Child of the Owl
Booklist 74 (1 April 1977): 1173.
Kingston, Maxine Hong. "Middle Kingdom to Middle America." *Book World—The Washington Post*, 1 May 1977.
Kirkus Reviews 45 (1 February 1977): 99.
Lewis, Marjorie. *School Library Journal* 23 (April 1977): 73.

The Curse of the Squirrel
Aswell, Joanne. *Kirkus Reviews* 55 (1 November 1987): 1582.
Hearne, Betsy. *Bulletin for the Center for Children's Books* 41 (November 1987): 60.
Kirkus Reviews 55 (1 November 1987): 1587.

Dragon of the Lost Sea
McKinley, Robin. *Voice of Youth Advocates* 5 (February 1983): 47.
Sutherland, Zena. *Bulletin of the Center for Children's Books* 36 (November 1982): 59–60.
Wilms, Denise M. *Booklist* 79 (1 October 1982): 250.

Dragon's Gate
Burns, Mary M. *Horn Book* 70 (March–April 1994): 208–9.
Chang, Margaret A. *School Library Journal* 40 (January 1994): 135.
Corsaro, Julie. *Booklist* 90 (1 January 1994): 817.

Dragon Steel
Sutherland, Zena. *Bulletin for the Review of Children's Books* 38 (May 1985): 178.
Taxel, Joel. *ALAN Review* 13 (fall 1985): 25.

Zeiger, Hanna B. *Horn Book* 61 (July–August 1985): 459–60.

Dragon War

Chang, Margaret A. *School Library Journal* 38 (June 1992): 144.

Smith, Candace. *Booklist* 88 (15 April 1992): 1524.

Sutherland, Zena. *Bulletin of the Center for Children's Books* 45 (April 1992): 226.

Dragonwings

Chin, Frank. *Interracial Books for Children Bulletin* 7:2,3 (1976): 25.

Gardner, Jane E. *School Library Journal* 22 (September 1975): 129.

Interracial Books for Children Bulletin 7:2,3 (1976): 9.

Pelmas, Ruth H. *New York Times Book Review*, 16 November 1975.

Kind Hearts and Gentle Monsters

Heins, Ethel. *Horn Book* 58 (June 1982): 302.

Rodowsky, Colby. *New York Times Book Review*, 23 May 1982.

Sutherland, Zena. *Bulletin of the Center for Children's Books* 35 (May 1982): 180.

Liar, Liar

Billman, Carol. *New York Times Book Review*, 6 November 1983.

Erbes, Bill. *Voice of Youth Advocates* 7 (April 1984): 37.

Wilms, Denise M. *Booklist* 80 (15 September 1983): 175.

The Lost Garden

Graham, Joyce, and Susan Murphy. *Journal of Reading* 36 (November 1992): 248.

Library Talk 6 (May 1993): 11.

Philbrook, John. *School Library Journal* 37 (August 1991): 208.

Rochman, Hazel. *Booklist* 88 (15 October 1991): 437.

Sutherland, Zena. *Bulletin of the Center for Children's Books* 45 (October 1991): 52.

The Man Who Tricked a Ghost

Booklist 89 (1 June 1993): 1835.

Burns, Mary M. *Horn Book* 69 (September 1993): 636.

Kirkus Reviews 61 (1 August 1993): 1010.

Loer, Stephanie. "Ghosts, Ghouls Overshadow Season's Selections." *Boston Globe*, 17 October 1993.

Publishers Weekly 240 (2 August 1993): 80.

School Library Journal 39 (September 1993): 227.

The Mark Twain Murders

Greenlaw, M. Jean. *ALAN Review* 10 (spring 1983): 19.

Stevenson, Drew. *School Library Journal* 28 (May 1982): 85.

Sutherland, Zena. *Bulletin of the Center for Children's Books* 35 (July–August 1982): 220.

Mountain Light
Cooper, Ilene. *Booklist* 82 (15 September 1985): 141.
McNamara, Shelley G. *School Library Journal* 32 (January 1985): 76.
Zipperer, Frank. *ALAN Review* 13 (spring 1986): 31.

The Rainbow People
Bulletin of the Center for Children's Books 42 (April 1989): 211.
Horn Book 65 (May–June 1989): 382.
Mellon, Constance A. *School Library Journal* 135 (May 1989): 123.

Sea Glass
Burns, Mary M. *Horn Book* 55 (October 1979): 542.
Forman, Jack. *School Library Journal* 26 (November 1979): 95.
Kao, Donald. *Interracial Books for Children Bulletin* 11 (1980): 16.

The Serpent's Children
Hammond, Nancy C. *Horn Book* 55 (August 1984): 479–80.
McConnell, Ruth M. *School Library Journal* 30 (August 1984): 88.
Sutherland, Zena. *Bulletin of the Center for Children's Books* 37 (March 1984): 138.

Shadow Lord
Rogow, Roberta. *Voice of Youth Advocates* 8 (August 1985): 195–96.
Stevens, W. D. "A Shadow of a Novel." *Fantasy Review* 8 (April 1985): 30.

The Shell Woman and the King
Booklist 89 (July 1993): 1973.
Bulletin of the Center for Children's Books 47 (October 1993): 63.
Kirkus Reviews 61 (15 August 1993): 1082.
Publishers Weekly 240 (12 July 1993): 79.

The Star Fisher
Burns, Mary M. *Horn Book* 67 (May/June 1991): 334.
Kozak, Carla. *School Library Journal* 37 (May 1991): 113.
Naylor, Alice Phoebe. *New York Times Book Review*, 13 October 1991.
Sutherland, Zena. *Bulletin of the Center for Children's Books* 44 (March 1991): 182.

Sweetwater
Booklist 70 (15 October 1973): 243.
Dodd, Wayne. *Children's Literature: Annual of The Modern Language Association Seminar on Children's Literature and The Children's Literature Association*, ed. by Francelia Butler, vol. 4 (1975), 173–74.
Green, William H. *Children's Literature: Annual of The Modern Language Association Seminar on Children's Literature and The Children's Literature Association*, ed. by Francelia Butler, vol. 5 (1976), 290.
Stableford, Brian. *Vector 78* (November–December 1976).

The Tom Sawyer Fires
Kolker, Sister Delphine. *Best Sellers* 44 (December 1984): 360.
Sutherland, Zena. *Bulletin of the Center for Children's Books* 38 (December 1984): 76.
Wilms, Denise M. *Booklist* 81 (1 October 1984): 253.

Tongues of Jade
Cooper, Ilene. *Booklist* 88 (15 December 1991): 757.
Hearne, Betsy. *Bulletin of the Center for Children's Books* 45 (November 1991): 80.
Philbrook, John. *School Library Journal* 37 (December 1991): 132.
Watson, Elizabeth S. *Horn Book* 68 (January–February 1992): 84.

Selected General Reference

Aoki, Elaine. "Turning the Page: Asian, Pacific American Children's Literature." In *Teaching Multicultural Literature*, ed. by Violet Harris. Norwood, Mass.: Christopher-Gordon Publishers, 1992, 109–36.

Bacon, Betty, ed. *How Much Truth Do We Tell the Children: The Politics of Children's Literature*. Minneapolis, Minn.: MEP Publications, 1988.

Chan, Jeffery Paul, Frank Chin, Lawson Fusao Inada, and Shawn H. Wong. "An Introduction to Chinese-American and Japanese-American Literatures." In *Three American Literatures: Essays in Chicano, Native American, and Asian-American Literature for Teachers of Literature*, ed. by Houston A. Baker Jr. New York: Modern Language Association, 1982, 197–228.

Chin, Frank, compiler. *Aiiieeeee: An Anthology of Asian-American Writers*. Washington, D.C.: Howard University Press, 1974.

Hong, Maria. *Growing Up Asian American: An Anthology*. New York: William Morrow, 1993.

Johnson, Dianne. *Telling Tales: The Pedagogy and Promise of African American Literature for Youth*. Westport, Conn.: Greenwood, 1990.

Kim, Elaine H. *Asian American Literature: An Introduction to the Writings and Their Social Context*. Philadelphia: Temple University Press, 1982.

Lee, Joann Faung Jean. *Asian Americans: Oral Histories of First to Fourth Generation Americans from China, the Philippines, Japan, India, the Pacific Islands, Vietnam and Cambodia*. New York: The New Press, 1981.

Lee, Sunyoung. "Books of Many Colors." *A. Magazine* 3:1 (1993): 34–35.

Lim, Shirley, and Mayumi Tsutakawa, eds. *The Forbidden Stitch: An Asian-American Women's Anthology*. Corvallis, Oreg.: Calyx Books, 1988.

Lim, Shirley, and Amy Ling, eds. *Reading the Literatures of Asian America*. Philadelphia: Temple University Press, 1992.

Mark, Diane Mei Lin, and Ginger Chih. *A Place Called Chinese America*. Dubuque, Iowa: Kendall/Hunt, 1982.

Perry, Theresa, and James W. Fraser, eds. *Freedom's Plow: Teaching in the Multicultural Classroom*. New York: Routledge, 1993.

Reed, Arthea J. S. *Reaching Adolescents: The Young Adult Book and the School*. New York: Merrill, 1994.

Rochman, Hazel. *Against Borders: Promoting Books for a Multicultural World*. Chicago: American Library Association, 1993.

Russell, David L. *Literature for Children: A Short Introduction*. New York: Longman, 1991.

Sadler, Glenn Edward, ed. *Teaching Children's Literature: Issues, Pedagogy, Resources*. New York: Modern Language Association, 1992.

Sims, Rudine. *Shadow and Substance: Afro-American Experience in Contemporary Children's Fiction*. Urbana, Ill.: National Council of Teachers of English, 1982.

Smith, Karen Patricia, ed. *Multicultural Children's Literature in the United States*. Winter 1993 issue of *Library Trends*. Champaign, Ill.: University of Illinois Graduate School of Library and Information Science, 1993.

"Truman Made Racist Remarks Throughout Life." *The State* (Columbia, S.C.), 25 October 1991.

Wong, Sau-ling Cynthia. *Reading Asian American Literature: From Necessity to Extravagance*. Princeton: Princeton University Press, 1993.

INDEX

The Author

Dianne Johnson-Feelings is an associate professor of English at the University of South Carolina, where she teaches courses in children's literature, young adult literature, and African-American literature. Among her publications is *Telling Tales: The Pedagogy and Promise of African American Literature for Youth*. She lives in her hometown of Columbia, South Carolina, with her husband, illustrator Tom Feelings, and daughter Niani Sekai.

The Editor

Patricia J. Campbell is an author and critic specializing in books for young adults. She has taught adolescent literature at UCLA and was formerly the assistant coordinator of young adult services for the Los Angeles Public Library. Her literary criticism has been published in the *New York Times Book Review* and many other journals. From 1978 to 1988 her column "The YA Perplex," a monthly review of young adult books, appeared in the *Wilson Library Bulletin*. She now writes a review column on the independent press for that magazine, and a column on controversial issues in adolescent literature for *Horn Book*. Campbell is the author of five books, among them *Presenting Robert Cormier*, the first volume in the Twayne Young Adult Authors Series. In 1989 she was the recipient of the American Library Association Grolier Award for distinguished achievement with young people and books. A native of Los Angeles, Campbell now lives on an avocado ranch near San Diego, where she and her husband, David Shore, write and publish books on overseas motorhome travel.